SEC 250

PERCEPTION, EMOTION AND ACTION:

A Component Approach

Library of Philosophy and Logic

General Editors:
P. T. Geach, J. L. Mackie, D. H. Mellor,
Hilary Putnam, P. F. Strawson, David Wiggins,
Peter Winch

LOGICAL INVESTIGATIONS
GOTTLOB FREGE
Translated by P. T. Geach and R. H. Stoothoff

GROUNDLESS BELIEF
MICHAEL WILLIAMS

PERCEPTION, EMOTION AND ACTION

A Component Approach

IRVING THALBERG

NEW HAVEN
YALE UNIVERSITY PRESS
1977

Printed in Great Britain

Contents

Acknowledgements

Professor Vivian M. Weil, from Illinois Institute of Technology, was co-author of the essay which is a primary source of chapter 5: "The Elements of Basic Action", published in *Philosophia* for January 1974. I thank the editors of that journal for letting me use the material here. Section 6 of 5 incorporates a few ideas from "When Do Causes Take Effect?", to appear in *Mind*, October 1975 —for which I thank the editor, as well as publishers Basil Blackwell & Mott. I am also grateful to them, and to the editor of *Analysis*, for allowing me to base chapter 1 upon my April 1973 article, "Ingredients of Perception". Chapter 3, and parts of 2 and 4 evolved from my "Constituents and Causes of Emotion and Action", which appeared in the January 1973 issue of *The Philosophical Quarterly*, whose editor I thank.

Audiences at various philosophical gatherings have helped me improve earlier versions of several chapters. I read the original of chapter 1 to the Canadian Philosophical Association in June 1972. Material from 2 and 3 was read to the Philosophy Collquium at Washington University in October 1972. Portions of 5 were presented to the Northwestern University Philosophy Club in November 1971, California State University at San Jose in October 1973, and University of Lethbridge (Canada) in March 1974.

Scattered criticisms of them notwithstanding, the most pervasive influences upon my thinking in philosophy of mind generally, and action theory specifically, have been Professors Donald Davidson and Roderick Chisholm. Although I doubt that either would agree with many of my conclusions and arguments, I am greatly indebted to both for patient discussions.

Last but not least, I heartily thank an anonymous reviewer from Blackwell's for scores of concrete suggestions on matters of style and argumentation.

Introduction

In this book I accept at face value a dozen rather befuddling controversies from the broad area which may be called philosophy of mind. Each chapter displays what we can do to put these quarrels to rest, and acknowledge the insights of major disputants, by deploying a relatively unhackneyed method of analysis. Each debate concerns the relationship between various sorts of events. Chapter 1 deals with three kinds of happening which coincide with the event of our perceiving some item. Thus I explore the relationship between seeing an object and (i) what takes place in the percipient's nervous system; (ii) the alleged appearance of sense-data before his mind; and (iii) the presence of whatever it is that he perceives. Here is a sample of the mysteries under debate: Does our perceiving consist in a brain process, or in our being afflicted with sense-data? Are these cerebral events and sensory images perhaps really all we perceive, or anyway all we can be certain of, when we seem to be aware of objects outside our bodies? Are such occurrences identical with the event of our perceiving? Might brain processes and sense-data instead be causes or effects of our perceiving? With regard to the external item we seem to perceive, how exactly can it bring about the event of our perceiving it? Can this be a causal relation at all? My component analysis provides straightforward and novel replies to these confusing questions.

Chapter 2 takes up a pair of similarly vexatious riddles

about the event of our undergoing an emotion, and the thinking upon which most of our affective attitudes are somehow 'based'. Incidentally, thinking which gives rise to emotion may be derived from—or indeed part of—our perceptual activity. An example would be one's thoughts while witnessing a catastrophe. At any rate, I ask whether there is a causal hookup between cognition and affect. Or is there instead an entailment between having an emotion that is 'directed' toward some object, and entertaining beliefs, doubts or conjectures about the object?

The second enigma I tussle with in this chapter goes back to Plato's *Philebus*. Take the special case where you are pleased, for example, that an old chum of yours has arrived in town. However, you happen to be mistaken in believing this. That is, your friend has not arrived. Consequently your pleasure is based on a false belief. Why shouldn't we agree with Plato that in such situations your pleasure is false as well? Is there any clear method of separating your emotion from the erroneous belief on which it is founded, so that we can confine falsity to the cognitive partner alone? Evidently a plausible treatment of the preceding general question about the 'based on' relationship between emotion and belief ought to have put us on the road toward settling this quandary over false pleasure.

There is more welcome overlap between the general issue about how our affective attitudes are grounded upon cognition, and the ferocious but stalemated dispute I face in Chapter 3. Here the question is: What does it mean to say that a man's action is based on reasons which he has to perform it? One point of intersection is that our thoughts as well as our resulting emotions may figure among our reasons for acting. As far as that goes, what we perceive may also furnish us grounds to act. Another link between the phenomena we are studying is that strictly 'conative' attitudes on which people act may be based upon their thinking, in the same way as their emotional attitudes. Lastly, we find the familiar champions of causality and of entailment locked in debate over the relationship between what a man does and his grounds for doing it. In this 'action and reasons' quarrel, as well as the 'emotion and thought' case, my 'component' approach opens up an alternative to both causal and entailment theories. Yet it preserves some of the most valuable *aperçus* from each of these contending accounts.

We leave the entailment-causality battle in chapter 4, but apostles of causation do not forsake us. Again I struggle with action—specifically with four long-standing mysteries: (i) Might our actions be nothing but movements of our bodies—perhaps caused by our desires and beliefs? (ii) Instead have our bodily movements nothing to do with our actions? (iii) How are the contractions of our muscles related to our deeds? and (iv) What bearing do processes in our central nervous system have upon our actions? My component analysis brings us to terms with a puzzle about the way our action must be caused by our beliefs and desires if it is to be intentional. We also deal with a beguiling argument which purportedly shows that our bodily motions are neither identical with, nor even part of, what we do. As for muscular contractions, I stalk a well-known paradox. It specifies that tensing and relaxing of our muscles both antedates and causes our act. But what if we perform the act precisely in order to get those contractions? If we say they result from the action, then since they are earlier, have we an instance of backwards causation here? A component analysis will dispel this appearance.

The last puzzle of this chapter brings us back to neurophysiology, which had threatened our assumptions about what it is to perceive an extra-bodily item. With regard to action, on the other hand, it has worried philosophers that neural processes always cause our decisions and deeds. Doesn't this deprive us of freedom in both spheres? A component approach reveals some confusions about what is supposed to cause what. It also helps us see that the operations of our nervous system when we decide and act cannot by themselves take away our liberty.

A more abstract metaphysical debate from action theory occupies my last and longest chapter. It develops from those common situations where we do one thing by means of doing another. For instance: a tired swimmer nears the shore by paddling; a gourmet summons the wine steward by raising his eyebrows vigorously; or, to fall back upon the sort of causal model which has almost uniquely preoccupied action theorists, a bus driver puts on the brakes by stretching out his right foot. I suggest a terminological convenience, to be justified later: whatever these people do with their bodies, as a means of achieving other results, we may call their basic actions. Whatever else they accomplish by thus moving all or part of their body will be a non-basic action. In circumstances where a person initiates one or more courses of non-basic action by performing a basic action, the philosophical debate is whether he carries out several distinct actions. Or does he only move his body in a way that, under the circumstances, has one or another consequence? Here we find Pluralists arrayed against Reductive Unifiers. The former discern a multiplicity of separate non-basic acts having their source in the agent's basic performance; while the latter see nothing but his basic act—thereby, of course, abolishing the basic/non-basic distinction. Predictably, my component analysis loosens this conceptual vise. Speaking roughly, it allows us to say both that the agent performs only one deed, and that he carries out non-basic as well as basic actions. When we set this out more fully, overtones of paradox will fade away.

A new worry may nag us after we run through my inventory of the elements of basic and non-basic action. I treat this in a brief epilogue. You might wonder if reasons for action, neural processes, muscular contractions and limb motions are all there is to agency. Is my list of components supposed to be an analysis of what it is for a person to act? If so, it seems to take away his initiative. He seems to be nothing but the arena in which desires, resolutions, emotions and beliefs either contend or blend with each other, finally producing agitation or stillness of his limbs. And if we try to put him back into the picture as agent, by emphasizing that it is he who engages in the mental activity which sets off the sequence of happenings, or analysis sounds like a Prichardian volition theory (see Prichard [1949], esp. p. 190). Obviously I want to avoid conceiving of the agent as the passive *locus* within which causes operate; and I also want to stay clear of Prichard's doctrine that, strictly speaking, what we really do is carry out acts of will. In outline, my solution to this dilemma will be to deny that elements of basic and non-basic action must constitute the 'essence' or 'nature' of action. At the same time I have to explain why it is nevertheless illuminating to regard these sub-events as components of what we do.

So much for my overall plan. I should say a few words to avert misunderstanding of what I am up to in general. First I shall clarify my position on the debates and puzzles to which my component theory is a response. When I struggled with four of them in a journal article, I seem to have misled some readers. In his subsequent commentary [1974], Mr Mitchell Straude appears to believe that I committed myself to a pair of quite extreme theses, namely: (a) that the enigmas I discuss are genuine, and formulated with sufficient clarity, as I present them; and (b) that my constituent analysis is the simplest, and also the only adequate treatment of these riddles. I think that nothing in my article implied acceptance of either (a) or (b). At any rate, in the following chapters I do not intend to assume (a) or (b). In fact I shall express occasional doubts whether the puzzles are meaningful and compelling. Also I shall try to make it plain that I deliberately examine them in their traditionally vague rhetorical guise. My rationale is that many leading philosophers have gotten deeply embroiled in controversy over these issues, and have stated them more or less as I do here. With regard to thesis (b) in particular, it would be incompatible with my explicit aim of giving each entrenched philosophical doctrine its due, whenever I can, if I accepted (b), and thought my approach the last and only word in metaphysical analysis of perceiving, belief, emotion, conation, action and similar occurrences.

I do not intend the component approach to be a definitive analysis of events. It is not my purpose to develop one here. In chapter 5, I do take a stand on how we should individuate events which are basic and non-basic actions. I am also especially critical of the Pluralists' general outlook. But my conclusions on individuation there, on the tie between reasons and deeds in chapter 3, and on the bodily components of action in chapter 4, leave me fairly neutral as to the 'essence' or 'intrinsic nature' of events and actions. In my epilogue, as noted, I deny that a list of the motivational, cerebral and large-scale bodily ingredients of a basic performance reveals any such occult item. But it would be a misunderstanding if readers thought that I harbored no prejudices about the nature of events and actions.

I lean heavily towards three doctrines which I find implicit in Davidson's work: (1) that events and actions are dated, non-repeatable particulars; (2) that the category of events is complementary to the category of physical objects which figure in events; (3) that although actions are classifiable as events, we cannot give any further analysis of what it is for something to be an event. It might be helpful if I explain why I favor (3), since many philosophers—mostly Pluralists—have offered, in Gold-man's words, to "lay bare the nature, or ontological status, of an act" ([1971], p. 768), and to say what makes something an event.

I am diffident toward these analyses not only because they support Pluralistic theories of act and event individuation. My main reason is that they seem ultimately to be circular, or to be uninformative technical stipulations. I constantly oscillate between these two suspicions; but when I read these analyses, I can find no third way of looking at them. I shall illustrate briefly. Brandt and Kim write, for example: "To say that there is an event of a certain kind is to say that some logically contingent property (set of properties) is instantiated at a specific time and 'location' " ([1967], p. 516). Along similar lines, R. M. Martin distinguishes three kinds of occurrence:

> Object-events are in effect enduring objects with the time of endurance made explicit. The cliffs-of-Dover-at-time-t constitutes an object-event.
>
> . . . Property-events . . . involve not only a physical object and a time, but also a property, or more parti-cularly, a property as relativized to a time . . . The eruption of Mt. Vesuvius involves not only Mt. Vesuvius, but the time of erupting . . .
>
> [The relational event] 'John's giving a ring to Mary' . . . involves the triadic relation of giving ([1969], pp. 66, 68, 69).

A more recent recipe of Kim's is that an event consists of "a concrete object (or n-tuple of objects) exemplifying a property (or n-adic relation) at a time. In this sense of 'event', events include states, conditions, and the like, and not only . . . changes" ([1973], p. 222; see pp. 219, 223-27; also his [1974], pp. 42, 45ff). Finally, Goldman declares: "Instead of treating action (or events) as a primitive or irreducible category, our account reduces act tokens [particular actions of a 'type'] to persons, act properties and times" ([1971], p. 773). More specifically: when "we say . . . 'John mowed his lawn', we assert that John exemplified the property of mowing his lawn"; consequently an "act token is . . . the exemplification of a property by an agent" ([1970], p. 10; see [1971], pp. 769-72).

The dilemma, 'Circular or merely stipulative?', becomes inescapable as soon as we think about the operative verb-phrases in these analyses. What is it for a property to be "instantiated"? We can skip Martin's "object-events", since they are simply objects. But how does the event of Mt. Vesuvius erupting "involve . . . a property" along with the volcano? What is it like for a concrete object or a person to go around "exemplifying" properties? The recurring prepositional phrase "at a time", and its equivalents, suggest that exemplifying, involvement and instantiation are themselves occurrences in which concrete physical items, people and detachable "properties" figure, for longer or shorter temporal periods. In everyday speech, when we praise a veteran soldier for exemplifying loyalty and courage throughout his service, we are concerned with an enduring, career-long event. Similarly, when a young woman gets involved in politics, or involved with an older married man, these are episodes of her life.

Perhaps we should not attach any philosophical significance to crude, ordinary speech. Instead we should think only of the axiomatic theories of events and actions in which these locutions are meant to be deployed. We forget ordinary meanings of the terms, and look exclusively at the formal definitions, formation rules, substitution rules, postulates and rules of inference. But then, although the analysis of events and actions will no longer seem circular, we will not be able to interpret its key terms at all, and we can hardly expect it to "lay bare the nature, or ontological status" of events and deeds.

My component approach offers no way around this dilemma, since it only enables us to specify sub-events which make up any particular event. That is because I developed it, not to uncover the essence of events generally, or action generally, but to reduce our bafflement over various kinds of occurrences which seem tied up with perception, emotion and behavior. I hope the component approach will yield therapeutic insight into other controversial goings-on besides those I discuss here. I am inclined to doubt that all happenings under the sun may be fruitfully divided into their sub-events, and so on *ad infinitum*. For that matter, I would feel uneasy about any philosophical notion, technique or principle which seemed to unravel every conceptual snarl and cool down all raging metaphysical debaters. But speaking positively, I think the virtue of a component approach is that it does less violence to facts upon which these puzzles are based than alternative theories I know; and perhaps not least that it allows us to attribute maximum cogency and truth to apparently incompatible positions.

To all these preliminaries, I should append one typographical clarification. I use quotation marks (",") only to cite the words of other writers and utterances I attribute to imaginary speakers. When I discuss words and sentences without attributing them to anyone, and when I use expressions—particularly philosophical jargon—ironically or hesitantly, I enclose them in single inverted commas (' , ').

1. Resolving Three Debates in Philosophy of Perception

I want to spin out a relatively novel account of what goes on when we perceive objects and occurrences. Aside from the freshness and simplicity of my 'component' analysis, its virtue is that it provides a niche for three troublesome kinds of events. These obviously have something to do with visual, auditory, tactile, olfactory and gustatory perception; but our handiest philosophical categories—cause-and-effect, identity—only compound our befuddlement about the relationship of these events to perceiving. I think my analysis gives them an honorable role, while rendering most of the interminable controversies over them altogether otiose. Naturally I expect my reasoning to pacify few of the entrenched debaters. Yet I hope it may discourage some unaligned philosophers from joining either of the bogged-down armies.

The goings-on which set off controversy are quite disparate: (i) electro-chemical happenings in our nervous system when we hear, touch, see, smell and taste; (ii) the putative cavalcade of auditory, tactile, visual, olfactory and gustatory sense data before our minds; (iii) the presence—or 'existence'— of a material object, or the unfolding of an occurrence, which is said to cause our perception of that object or occurrence.

For brevity, I follow tradition and concentrate on seeing. I use that term broadly, to cover active scanning, passive gaping, careful and inattentive observing, successful spotting, along with most forms of visual misperceiving. I must neglect those varieties of perceiving and misperceiving where no publicly visible object or event is within range. Hence my analysis will not apply straightforwardly to hallucinatory perceiving. Space does not allow me to explain why a percipient is active in some kinds of seeing. I apologize as well for my hasty and uncritical résumés of philosophical debate over neuron firings, sense-data, and object-causes of seeing. My intention is to keep out of these wrangles.

(1) ARE WE ONLY AWARE OF OUR OWN BRAIN PROCESSES WHEN WE PERCEIVE?

Controversy about neural events only heated up during the past century, as physiologists learned that electrochemical goings-on in our optic nerve, and other regions of our cerebral cortex, are indispensable to sight. When these processes are impeded, our visual activities halt. Moreover, experimenters can demonstrate that when they subject a person's brain to the right electrical stimulation, he will swear that he sees objects and events. Yet no corresponding items are before him. His testimony is less significant, however, than the fact that occurrences in his central nervous system at the time resemble those which take place when suitable objects and events are on view.

Since these brain processes appear to play a leading role in our perceptual undertakings, philosophers have wondered: Is sight perhaps nothing but the firing of neurons? Bertrand Russell's hypotheses were more audacious. In *Outline of Philosophy* [1927], he maintained that what you see, and all you ever see, are the sensory terminals of your own brain! He declared: "All that you see must count as inside your body" (p. 146; compare pp. 131f, 135f, 138f, 140, 144f, 148f). Elsewhere in the same book, Russell modified his doctrine to something like this: All you know for sure, when you engage in perceptual adventures, is that some characteristic neural process is occurring. There may be no material object facing you, and your sense organs may not be functioning. But whatever tricks are being played upon you, you can be sure that your neurons are firing. So even if we are not perceptually aware of processes within our skull—since we do not witness them—these are all we have certain knowledge of when we see.

From the opposing side, down-to-earth philosophers may take just as paradoxical a view, and deny that neural events have anything to do with sight. Isn't it conceivable that human beings should see but have no nervous system at all, and therefore shelter no electro-chemical activity within their skulls? More cautiously, one might adapt some points considered by J. J. C. Smart in another context:

> It is only a contingent fact (if it is a fact) that when we have a certain kind of sensation there is a certain kind of process in our brain. Indeed it is possible . . . that our present physiological theories will be as out of date as the ancient theory connecting mental processes with goings-on in the heart ([1959], p. 58).

> [An expert in neurophysiology] can talk quite happily about his aches, . . . perceptions, . . . thoughts, and so on, with someone who does not know anything at all about brains, or who, like Aristotle, thinks that it is an organ for cooling the blood ([1972], p. 149)

The challenge to Russell's view is simple. How can he claim to know with certainty of these cerebral processes? Logically and epistemically speaking, they seem inessential to perception.

The upshot of this debate is that apparently we must equate seeing with neural activity, or else recognize two entirely independent realms of sight and the brain. Either we are perceptually confined to our own cerebral cortex, and shut off from the material world around us; or else we dismiss empirical investigation of what goes on in our nervous system as not germane to seeing!

My component analysis of perception takes us between these dialectical horns. Instead of reducing your visual exploits to neuron firing, we say that this cerebral occurrence is one ingredient of a broader event: your seeing an object outside of your cranium. Pending further clarification in subsequent chapters (especially throughout 4, and sections 3, 5-13 of 5), I offer two analogies in the hope of conveying my notion of what it is for one event to be part of another. First, think of what happens when an outboard motor runs. The engine itself is made up of moving parts, *inter alia*. It is not something extra alongside them. The event of the motor's operating consists in the sparkplug's firing, the combustion of air and gas inside the cylinder, the movement of pistons, valves and so forth. No sub-event by itself constitutes the engine's operating; nor is the latter an additional occurrence, over and above the sub-events which compose it.

Notice also that these component happenings are not mere segments of a broader occurrence. A temporal segment would be the first hour of the engine's break-in period. For a contrasting spatial slice, we might think of a lawn sprinkler which constantly sprays the back yard. Then we can divide its performance into the watering of the north side of the yard and the watering of the south side. At any rate, temporal and spatial slices of a larger event differ from a component inasmuch as they are homogeneous with the occurrence of which they are

THREE DEBATES OVER PERCEPTION   15

fractions. The first hour of the break-in is an operating of the engine; the spraying of the north end of a yard is a spraying. But a component of the engine's operating, such as the firing of a sparkplug, is not an operating of an engine.

My second model, from the human sphere, is group behaviour. For a concrete example of collective action, take an urban uprising. The ingredients of a particular revolt might be: Harry smashing windows, Bill setting fire to the unoccupied Welfare office, Mary inscribing 'All power to the people!' upon a tenement wall, Sam breaking open the corner grocery, Policeman Friendly blasting away with dum-dum bullets, and so on for at least a hundred participants. None of these individual antics will qualify as the urban rebellion. Yet the uprising is not a further occurrence alongside, or mysteriously caused by, the individual deeds which composed it. Again we easily distinguish constituent events from temporal and spatial segments—the intensified disorders following the arrival of National Guard troops, or what happened east of Broadway, both of which are themselves uprisings.

Shortly we shall register dissimilarities between seeing, with its neural event component, and these two cases. But first we need some terminology. It is obvious that an urban insurrection must encompass some forms of agressive behavior by many residents. Nevertheless those concrete acts we listed did not have to occur. Yet if a revolt occurred in Ghettoville, doesn't it follow logically that there were some individual deeds of the sort we catalogued? There would have been no revolt unless a minimal number of inhabitants carried out acts which authorities had forbidden them to perform. Incidentally, some of these individual acts may have begun before the rebellion itself. For example, Harry may have been on a window-breaking spree since the previous day. His vandalism, however, did not start to be part of the uprising until today, when there were enough other individual acts going on around him to constitute, along with his window-smashing today, a rebellion. In other words, his shattering of windows yesterday was not part of an insurrection, because none was going on yesterday. For parallel reasons, an individual caper which is now part of the up-rising may outlast the collective frenzy—that is, may con-tinue after the majority of insurgents have been quelled.

Now my first terminological move is to distinguish between individual deeds of various types, such that a fair number had to occur if there was to be an urban uprising, and other acts which were part of the revolt. We can call the former logically *necessary* component events, and the latter *accidental*. An instance of the latter would be Officer Friendly's gunfire. This does not mean that he shot by accident—only that there does not have to be shooting by authorities in order for there to be an urban uprising. So an accidental ingredient is simply an event of some type which need not occur whenever a broader occurrence of a given kind takes place.

This distinction is rooted in our event-language alone. Over television, or on the scene, Harry's window-breaking spree will not look to you any more 'logically necessary' than the patrolman's gunplay. In fact, this 'accidental' component, in spite of its humble logical status, may be more noteworthy from a 'dynamic' or causal standpoint; for it may have either deterred or maddened the in-surgents.

This brings me to a second terminological move. Officer Friendly's gunfire, along with the other sub-events I have catalogued thus far, I label 'causal ingredients'. What would be a non-causal component? Imagine that an isolated rebel is singing. It does not matter what else he is up to. Suppose that he is singing from habit—or training, if precision is needed. Thus his current vocal endeavors did not result from the rebellious behavior of fellow ghetto residents, and his singing does not influence them. By contrast with causal event-components, whether logically necessary or accidental, we might dub this solitary outburst of song a mere 'accompaniment' of the ghetto uprising.

Next I want to distinguish between causal components of a larger event, whether accidental or necessary, and those events which caused it. Antecedent or simultaneous occurrences which helped bring about, exacerbate or cool the uprising may not figure among its ingredients. Suppose that a community leader was assassinated yesterday, and that this precipitated, although it was not part of, the insurrection which began today. Why wasn't this a component? Because the population was calm yesterday, at the time an assailant surprised the community leader. Other events which might have an influence on the revolt, without being part of it, would be decisions by faraway non-participants which may bring about a sharpening or else a cessation of rebellion in the ghetto.

One last remark on terminology: If we glance back to the outboard motor example, we appreciate how arbitrary the 'necessary'/'accidental' dichotomy can be. Suppose the motor is running. Does it follow logically that the engine has a sparkplug, and that the sparkplug ignites periodically? Does combustion have to take place? Must there be any internal goings-on at all for the engine to operate? Perhaps all that is required is the propeller's turning? Evidently we lack a precise definition of what it is for an engine to operate. My feeling in this case is that we would waste our time deciding whether to tag some of these component occurrences as either necessary or accidental sub-events. But causal ingredients are in a different situation. Ordinary empirical investigation will reveal the degree to which any sub-event is determined by an earlier or a simultaneous component, and what influence a sub-event has upon other component occurrences.

Can I encapsulate all this into a statement of logically necessary and sufficient conditions—a definition of what it takes for one event to be part of another? That would not be my style; and in any case I have no recipe for picking out sub-events which make up a larger occurrence. But is this any problem? As the illustrations I've given reveal, we do pick out sub-events with ease. It helps us do so if we understand the meanings of event-words. Common sense and scientific training also facilitate our task. Specifically, we have no difficulty in practice distinguishing events which are causal components, say of the motor's operation, from other events which cause the motor to operate—for instance, the motion of its starter cable. Moreover, we seldom hesitate to say when an event or its components have begun, when they are over, and when their effects—such as water pollution from the outboard engine—are occurring instead.

Now we must return to our original puzzlement about the relationship between seeing and having certain processes occur in our brain. Our mechanical and social models diverge only slightly from this problem case. According to what most speakers mean by the verb 'see', those mysterious happenings in the percipient's optic nerve and cerebral cortex are not logically necessary ingredients of seeing. But physiologists have demonstrated their causal preeminence, from the moment light strikes our retina.

You might admit that changes in our optic nerve result from chemical processes involving the rods and cones of our eye, but ask what effects neural happenings bring about. Maybe they trigger sense data. We shall consider that riddle soon enough. Another possibility is that neural events cause beliefs to arise in the perceiver's mind regarding objects and events around him. Such beliefs, incidentally, normally figure as necessary components of perceiving. I say "normally" because I want to leave it open whether there are cases of 'seeing but disbelieving' and 'seeing but not registering'. Apart from such questions, we still face a difficulty over belief components. For if mind-body 'identity' theorists are right—a point which will come up repeatedly throughout this book—then my believing would be the same event as some process in my brain when I see. Therefore my believing could not be an effect of, and entirely separate from, brain-process components; and the latter would be without cognitive components as their effects. Now the hitch, for my analysis, is that if partisans of identity are correct, then the same component is and is not logically necessary to seeing. But the contradiction evaporates as soon as we recall that 'necessary componency' is language-dependent. Labelled as an instance of my believing that q, event E is a logically necessary ingredient of my seeing X. Tagged as a neural process, E is not. So if E is both a neural happening and an instance of my believing that q, our only fault is that we have recorded a single component twice. Here is a parallel. We attend a committee meeting. Louise is there. We describe her as 'the tallest woman in the room' and as 'the committee chairperson'. Under the first description she is not, while under the second she is necessarily a member of the committee.

I realize that there are many residual obscurities regarding *what* one must believe when one sees an object or event X. I need not resolve these uncertainties in order to dismiss the debate we began with over perception and neural happenings. In terms of that problem, what matters is that my component analysis will not allow us to identify the 'larger' event of our perceiving X and the brain process which is one of its ingredients. In other words, we should be able to resist the temptation to hold that seeing is nothing but a neural process. Equally important, we shall be discouraged from saying that neural events cause 'the perception'—cause us to see X. What goes on beneath our cranium is a constituent of our seeing X. It makes no more sense to claim that the neural sub-event brought about our seeing than it does to say an individual looter's activity caused the rebellion in which he was participating. What does cause us to see objects and events? That will be our third problem, after we grapple with sense-data.

Before we move on, I ought to summarize how my analysis puts to rest our worries over brain processes. My results are mainly negative, but still quite therapeutic: As I've noted, visual perception is not reducible to its neural component. Such neural happenings may be, or may not be, identical with the percipient's having sense-data, or his having beliefs about nearby objects and events. That is, my account is compatible with, but does not entail a mental-neural identity thesis. Finally there is no danger any more that brain processes which occur when we see will deny us access to objects we look at. The neural event will not be what we see, but a vital component of our seeing objects, due to its importance as an effect of light rays striking our eye.

(2) DO WE ONLY PERCEIVE OUR SENSE DATA?

Now we must confront items which physiologists seem barred from examining, by microscope or electro-encephalogram. Still! it is a natural transition from brain processes to sense impressions. Many philosophers assimilate sense data to the last events which occur in our brain whenever we perceive. Dualistically inclined metaphysicians imagine that the firing of our neurons mysteriously coincides with, or perhaps brings about, the intrusion of visual images upon our mind. In the book I cited, Russell himself slides away from his argument that a physiologist with another's brain before him can only peer at the sensory terminals of his own cortex. Soon Russell is maintaining: "In the strict sense, a physiologist cannot observe anything in the other brain he is examining; but only the percepts [sense data] which he himself has when hs is suitably related to that brain" ([1927], p. 147).

I won't evaluate Russell's or any other writer's methods of proving that we have "percepts", no doubt upon something akin to an internal cinema screen—when we are beset with after-images, when we undergo optical illusions, when we hallucinate, or maybe whenever we see. Most beginning philosophy students and laymen with whom I've discussed perception seem predisposed to report items of this kind 'in here', entering and leaving their visual field. Why should we declare they cannot have them?

Of course I am tempted to put forth challenges: Can you show me a sense datum—or at least give me some identifying marks so that I will be able to fish one out of my own stream of consciousness? For that matter, where exactly is this stream or field they inhabit? How can you determine when a particular sense datum begins and ceases to exist there? Can it exist outside the stream? Turning to other details, I would ask if your visual images have spatial dimensions like depth. How do you measure these dimensions? What of qualities like weight and temperature? Presumably sense data have color and shape; but do they come to have these qualities in the way a leaf or wood-carving does? Generally, how do you get into contact with a sense datum? Do you see it? With what? Are there ideal or minimal conditions for viewing it? Will any circumstances prevent you from getting a complete and accurate look?

If some theorist cagily rules that we just 'sense' a sense datum, I would ask him for instructions in this new activity of sensing. If his next defensive reply is that it is more correct to say we 'have' sense data, I would demand an account of this peculiar kind of ownership. Some philosophical super-scientists will majestically brush aside these crude questions, and say that we should regard a sense datum as a 'theoretical entity', on a par with electrons and pi-mesons. I admit that it would be inappropriate to make such inquiries about electrons. Although I'm intimidated by this invocation of science, my curiosity remains. What parity is there between electrons and sense impressions? What cloud chambers, mathematical procedures or crucial observations make it reasonable for you to posit sense data? How can invisible, unsensed and unowned electrons be like visual images, which are somehow known or possessed by one percipient alone?

I pose questions like these out of compassion for anti-sense-datum philosophers, who worry that our sense data will block off 'external objects'. This would indeed be a consequence if we held that all you are aware of during perception is what crops up in your visual field. A further complaint would be that a sense datum theory makes perception immune to scientific study. Yet I am also torn the other way. Simply to deny the existence of sense impressions would, for many ordinary thinking people and venerable philosophers, amount to denying the obvious.

Again my component analysis takes us around the dilemma. If you are deeply attached to your visual field and its flora, keep them. In your case, the event of receiving an image of a dragonfly will be one constituent of your watching the dragonfly circle overhead. Your scrutinizing, or gaping at, the dragonfly is not reducible to this sense datum component. And it would be a gross *non sequitur* if you concluded that the only object or event you see—all you are aware of—is this sense datum ingredient. Even if you insist on claiming knowledge of your sense impressions, you may still claim knowledge of the dragonfly 'out there' in addition. Is it not what you see, however deviously? Perhaps you are one of those individuals who are beseiged by sense data when you watch things like this dragonfly. Nevertheless you manage to keep the dragonfly in sight! One last advantage of interpreting sense data as components of perception is that you are free to identify your visual images with brain process components, or to indulge in mental-physical dualism. Moreover, two forms of separatism are possible. You can try to establish causal interaction between brain process and sense datum components. Or you can record regular coincidences between sub-events of these ontologically disparate kinds. If you take an interactionist view, sense data would be causal components. If your approach is parallelist, sense data would have no tie with physical components of one's seeing, but they would have an effect upon one's mental state of believing that object X is present, or that event E is occurring in one's neighborhood.

If we hark back to the other distinction I made with respect to neural happenings, we may encounter some trouble deciding whether sense data are logically necessary constituents of sight. Presumably not. Many people, like myself, only think they may have sense data when they get after-images or 'see stars'—not straightforward cases of seeing an object or event. And most sense-datum philosophers introduce visual images by means of the so-called

Argument from Illusion. They write as if it were an empirical discovery, like those about the optic nerve, that sense data blossom in our visual field when we misperceive things, such as the proverbial oar halfway immersed in water. Yet a few proponents of the Argument from Illusion, and some plain folk, seem to take it for granted, *a priori*, that we have sense data whenever we see. For such thinkers, the issue is only whether we are ever entitled to claim perceptual knowledge of anything beyond our ever-present sense impressions. Here I'm afraid my component analysis simply rules out the 'logically necessary' approach to sense data. But isn't such arbitrariness a low price to pay for an analysis which allows the devotee of visual impressions to introduce them, without suffering any consequences feared by anti-sense-datum writers?

(3) DO THINGS WE PERCEIVE CAUSE US TO PERCEIVE THEM?

The third controversial item on my schedule is the object or event we see. According to adherents of the Causal Theory of Perception (CTP), one thing we mean by 'see an object' is that the object figured somehow as a cause of our seeing it. Professor Grice formulates this far more subtly. In his essay which revived debate over the CTP, we read:

> [It is] insufficient merely to believe that the perception of a material object is always to be causally explained by reference to conditions the specification of at least one of which involves a mention of the object perceived . . . This appears to be a very general contingent proposition; though . . . if the version of the CTP with which I shall be primarily concerned is correct, it (or

something like it) will turn out to be a necessary rather than a contingent truth . . . It may be held that the elucidation of the notion of perceiving a material object will include some reference to the role of the material object perceived in the causal ancestry of the perception (or of the sense impression or sense datum involved in the perception). This contention is central to what I regard as a standard version of the CTP. ([1961], p. 85)

Nuances notwithstanding, I am unsure what Grice means by "the perception". Ultimately he focusses on "the sense impression or sense datum involved in the perception". Apparently Grice believes that the English phrase, 'It looks to me as if there were an X before me', may serve to report a speaker's visual sense datum. If we reject that questionable assumption, and distinguish between 'It looks to me as if there were an X before me' and 'The object before me looks to me as if it were an X', then we have four versions of the CTP. Deploying my tired dragonfly example again, and speaking unidiomatically, we get:

(i) I see the dragonfly (circling above me) as a result of its presence (because it is circling above me);

(ii) The object overhead looks to me as if it were a dragonfly, as a result of its being a dragonfly (because it is one);

(iii) It looks to me as if there is a dragonfly overhead, and this is a result of the dragonfly's presence overhead;

(iv) I have a dragonfly sense datum in my visual field, as a result of the dragonfly's aerial activity.

Can we elaborate any of these variants so as to make it clear that the dragonfly's presence brings about my seeing the dragonfly? Seemingly with (iii) and (iv) both in mind, Grice offers this hint:

> the best procedure for the Causal Theorist is to indicate the mode of causal connection by examples; to say that, for an object to be perceived by X, it is sufficient that it should be causally involved in the generation of some sense impression by [sic] X in the kind of way in which, for example, when I look at my hand in good light, my hand is causally responsible for its looking to me as if there were a hand before me, or in which . . . (and so on), *whatever that kind of way may be*; and to be enlightened on that question one must have recourse to the specialist. ([1961], p. 105)

Whether or not we confound versions (i) through (iv), we shall hear vigorous outcries against the CTP. Here is a sampling: Suppose it is true that when we explain my seeing the dragonfly, the dragonfly should come into the explanation. But don't we beg the question under debate if we just assume that the explanation here must be causal? What marks it as one? Can we list any well established causal laws relating the presence of such objects to our catching sight of them, or their looking some way to us? Hardly: instead we find laws correlating the presence of such objects and the propagation of light rays from the object, and both with subsequent changes of the perceiver's retina; and so on. When we investigate the causes of perceiving and misperceiving objects, we never learn of the object's presence. Instead we study the favorable and unfavorable influence of illumination, backdrop, distance, camouflage, fog. We establish optimum and hindering conditions of the percipient: previous training, enthusiasm, expectations, myopia, fatigue, suggestibility. If these are the determinants of our perceptual successes and shortcomings, and of how an object looks to us, then versions (i) and (ii) of the CTP lose plausibility. The causes of my seeing the dragonfly, and of the object over-head looking to me like a dragonfly, do not include the dragonfly itself.

With regard to version (iii), as well as (ii), Professor Alan White airs the following doubts:

> [It] is an analytically true statement that the word 'goal' (a snake, a bush) looks to normal persons in normal conditions as if it were, e.g., the word 'goal' (a snake, a bush) . . . Grice's view that the explanation of its here and now looking to me as if there were the word 'goal,' in terms of the presence of the word 'goal', is of a causal kind would only follow if the non-contingent statement, that its looking to a normal person as if there were an X is in normal conditions due to the presence of an X, expresses a causal law . . . But . . . I am inclined to say that no statement of a causal law can be non-contingent. Further, is it not the case that, *if* the cir-cumstances are normal, then not only does X look as if it were an X, but also it looks as if there were an X [and] there is an X? ([1961], pp. 120-121)

What if circumstances or the perceiver's condition are abnormal instead? Then those untoward factors would causally account for the dragonfly looking to me like a tiny grey desert bat, and for its looking to me as if there is a desert bat overhead. How about the involuted case where I overcome conditions of myself or my sur-roundings which make dragonflies strongly resemble desert bats? Then whatever enables me to rise above per-ceptual temptation must be the cause of its looking to me, in spite of everything, as if there is a dragonfly overhead. This vehicle of epistemic grace cannot be the dragonfly itself. So far, then, we have tried three versions of the CTP, but we have discovered to reason to accept it so far.

A further grumble against interpretation (iii) is that the key phrase, 'It looks to me as if there is a dragonfly', is not as a rule used to assert, even guardedly, that one has *seen* a dragonfly. Normally one thereby expresses an estimate or belief, not necessarily based on perceiving the object in question. An example would be: 'It looks to me as if another monetary crisis has begun.' If defenders of the CTP agree, then variant (iii) is no more than a causal theory of how objects determine one's beliefs about one's immediate surroundings, where these may or may not be beliefs about what one currently sees. In terms of my component analysis, (iii) records a causal relationship between an object and the cognitive ingredients of my seeing it, not between object and seeing.

As a causal hypothesis about our dragonfly's effect upon the whole event of my seeing the dragonfly, interpretation (iv) must be disqualified on similar grounds. We noticed earlier why it is implausible to equate the events of perceiving X and having Xish sense data. So at best, (iv) illustrates how the sense-datum component of my seeing the dragonfly results from the dragonfly's aerial caper: hardly an instance of X causing perception of X.

Faithful to my pledge of neutrality, I will not attempt to vindicate defenders or enemies of the CTP. From my remarks on variants (iii) and (iv) of that embattled doctrine, it should be obvious how I plan to arrange a truce. It does sufficient honor to the CTP if we say: The dragonfly's presence causes light rays to strike my retina, bringing about chemical transformations in the rods and cones of my eye; this sends electrical impulses along my optic nerve. Further effects would be certain states of my cortex; my new belief that a dragonfly or some insect is overhead; and—if I am blessed with them—a fresh harvest of sense impressions in my visual field. The creature's hovering causes, either proximately or indirectly, each of these occurrences. Does it bring about the composite event of my seeing the dragonfly? This is not a logical consequence. But if we draw such a conclusion anyway, then we have to deal with the objections I noted against 'holistic' readings of the CTP—namely (i), (ii) and perhaps (iii).

On my analysis, the dragonfly's hovering is not just a cause of these other components of seeing the dragonfly. It is an ingredient too. Does that sound outrageous? Not if you reflect on what I'm asserting. To say the dragonfly's presence is part of my seeing is not to say that it is present in me—somehow part of me! That would follow only if you assume, question-beggingly, that the event of my seeing X must somehow be confined to me. But why underline the possessive pronoun here? Isn't it more correct to hold that N's perceiving X is a relational event involving N and X? Relational occurrences, like X drifting above N, do not take place 'in' X or N. Our feeling of outrage diminishes further if we review what happens when people are perceptually related to objects. For one thing, it must be the case that X is along N's line of sight. If N has mirrors, the line may be crooked. All this suggests that 'I see the dragonfly overhead' entails 'The dragonfly is overhead.' Its presence, in this sense, is a logically necessary component of my seeing it, as well as a cause of other subevents.

Scientific and common sense investigation are bound to reveal other ingredients of perception besides light waves and the three philosophically worrisome elements I have discussed. Historians learn more about what happened during an urban insurrection. Mechanics discover new details of an engine's operation. I have offered no criteria, much less logically necessary or sufficient conditions, for saying what sub-events make up some type of occurrence. Neither do social scientists and garage-men.

One risk of proceeding so informally is that I may have no way of excluding any item as a constituent of some event like my perceiving the dragonfly. Without the earth's motion during the past twenty-four hours, or for that matter the formation of the solar system five billion years ago, would I have been able to see the dragonfly? No; but earlier I sharply distinguished such causes of my current perceptual activity from its causal or non-causal components. So while I admit that I *may* have left the door open to unwanted components, not every causally contributing event will intrude.

Still thinking cosmically, as objector might bring up the old riddle of my spotting an extra-galactic nebula which exploded millenia ago, although its light is just reaching me now. Did the event of my seeing the nebula begin so long before I was born? One reply would be that such events take such a long time that they have to start before the lucky observer's birth. But I'm unsure that the question is clear enough to merit a simple answer. What about Einstein on simultaneity? Is it correct to assume that the nebula blew up at the same time as events which were taking place on earth thousands of years ago? A third reply is that the time lag puzzle is no more damaging to my component analysis of perceiving than to any alternative theories.

My goal in propounding this analysis was to clarify the status of neural goings-on, sense data and less arcane objects which we feel are somehow tied up with perceiving. I've concentrated on avoiding stalemated disputes. Nevertheless my ingredient analysis is compatible with a wide range of metaphysical positions. You can be an identity theorist about sense impressions and beliefs; or you can be a dualist of either parallelist or inter-actionist leanings. Most important, you can assume that there are objects to be seen, which affect us when we see them.

2. A Pair of Riddles about Emotion

I shall have no more to say on problems of perception; but the rest of this inquiry will be devoted to similar tangles in philosophy of mind, narrowly speaking, which I hope will yield to a component analysis. I turn first to a very general problem, which has some obvious affinities with the last debate about perception that we considered. There the Causal Theory of Perception was at issue. We felt inclined to suppose that our perceptual activity must be somehow causally dependent upon the object or event we perceive. In regard to emotional attitudes and responses, doesn't it seem plausible to suppose that they have causal ties to the situations, events or things which they are 'about'?

Not quite, perhaps. Imagine that I am terrified of a frothing Doberman Pincher. Another way of depicting my emotion would be to say that the dog's slobbering, snarling and barking frightens me. But could it possibly be true to say of me that I am afraid of this canine, or its menacing behavior, if I am totally unaware of the beast's presence? Clearly not. Surely I must have seen it, heard it, or heard about it from someone, if I am frightened of it. Even if I shut my eyes in terror, and cover my ears, I must believe it is in the vicinity, if I fear it. Incidentally, if the animal's carryings-on merely affected my visual apparatus—the rods and cones of my eyes, my optic nerve—but I was not attentive enough for it to 'register', then also I could not be said to cower in fear of that dog. Its activity must cause me to believe it is there, that it is dangerous, and so on, at a minimum. The upshot of this example is that if an object or event is causally related to some emotion I feel toward the object or event, then my thinking about the object or event must mediate. This is equally true when I perceive the item. So the tie which interests me here is between emotion and cognition, rather than between emotion and the 'object' of both emotion and thought.

What sort of connection do we envisage when we assume that a person's emotional attitude toward O is 'based' on his thinking about O? This is a doubly challenging analytic task because some eminent philosophers have become convinced that the bond is logical, and for that reason cannot be causal. Thus we have a debate between such 'entailment' theorists and partisans of causality, with common sense apparently on the side of the latter. Among defenses of an entailment view I would list Bedford, "Emotions" and Ryle, "Pleasure", both reprinted in Gustafson [1964]; the essays by Williams, Penelhum and myself in Hampshire [1966]; and Kenny's book [1963], chapters I-VI. Recent arguments for a causal interpretation are Armstrong [1968], pp. 179-86; and Wilson [1972], which I examined in detail elsewhere [1974].

In this debate I shall again deploy the method I just used to clarify the role in perception of cerebral goings-on, sense data and the items we perceive. Again I shall look for a reasonable compromise. In the process of negotiating a truce between champions of entailment and of causality, we shall probably gain a deeper appreciation of the phenomena under debate. As before, I leave it an open question whether the phenomena I discuss in the 'mentalistic' patois of cognition and affect are in fact, though obviously not by definition, also physical events.

That should be enough background for our first puzzle about the tie between someone's emotion that H—where the schematic letter 'H' stands for the object of his emotion—and his thinking that H, upon which we say his emotion is somehow 'based' or 'grounded'. An example of emotion that H might be a tourist's sudden anxiety that he has mislaid his passport. Should we suppose that his troubled state has resulted, in an ordinary causal sense, from his belief or conjecture that he misplaced the document? Or is such thinking instead a logically necessary condition for undergoing the sort of emotion we attribute to him? Then if we accept the Humean principle that only logically distinct items may be causally related, we are in a bind. Surely what a person believes, doubts, or 'wonders' must have an effect upon his moods. This seems self-evident to non-philosophers and to philosophical friends of causality alike. On the other hand, if we reflect a moment we seem to discern more than a contingent connection here. Can we imagine a woman being thrilled that her nephew won a Rhodes scholarship, yet having no idea that he is a candidate, much less a winner? Now if cognitive states or episodes like these were only causes, there would be no contradiction in supposing that she underwent this emotion and harbored no thoughts at all. Alternatively, it should be conceivable that her delight over her nephew's good fortune resulted only from irrelevant thoughts—only from her belief, say, that inflation has gotten worse.

Nor is this the end of our dispute. According to some entailment theorists, emotion that H requires more than just thinking that H. In their view, each standard form of emotion is linked with a specific kind or range of cognition. Thus it would be logically impossible that the woman should be overjoyed by her nephew's honor while firmly doubting or merely conjecturing that he received the award. Conversely, if her emotion is just wishing that he would get it, she cannot now be convinced by overwhelming evidence that he has been selected.

Both causal and entailment doctrines sound reasonable. If we invoke the 'cause'-'constituent' distinction, we won't have to take sides, or deny any leading facts adduced by either party. To votaries of causation we grant that your thinking that H—or its cerebral counterpart—may have innumerable effects. Nevertheless, with respect to the total episode of your emotion that H, your thinking is not a cause but an ingredient. Using the terminology of chapter 1, we can dub thinking that H a logically necessary component of emotion that H. Naturally the whole event of your undergoing the emotion that H, as well as its cognitive ingredient, have causes. And your thinking is a causal component. Other elements of the total occurrence, some of them logically necessary and some accidental, may be influenced by your thinking, or by its neural equivalent: for instance such elements as your blood pressure, adrenalin flow and breathing rate.

Having said this to causationists, what shall we concede to partisans of entailment? Various consequences of *describing* events *as* emotional episodes. For example, from the report that you are undergoing the emotion that H, obviously we can deduce that you think that H. We would not have had a case of the woman rejoicing over her nephew's triumph if she were in ignorance of the whole business. Our tourist cannot be worried about his passport while having no thoughts regarding it. But against entailment theorists we must point out that there are many other available descriptions for these episodes which lack 'cognitive' implications. We can single out and delineate many details of the tourist's fretting, or the woman's rejoicing, without using emotion terminology. We can report an event which is an outburst of emotion *while not stating that it is*, or 'over what' it occurred. For instance, we limit ourselves to an inventory of the tourist's frowning, sighing and cursing. From this story of the episode, you might guess that he is worried, and that he believes his passport is lost. But the report does not specify that he is anxious, or imply anything about his cognitive state. It's as if a gardener told you the size, shape, weight and color of a rock he dug up. What he described is in fact a Hopi Indian tombstone, although he has not so described it. His report, unlike the report of an archeologist, does not entail that the stone is a grave-marking device. Both specifications enable us to pick out the item from surrounding objects, and tell us what sort of thing it is. Depending upon our practical and theoretical interests, we will rate one description as more complete or informative than the other.

Of course entailment theorists are primarily concerned with the 'objects' of those events which are episodes of emotion—and justifiably so, because people's emotions are usually *about* things. As soon as we spell out what frightens, irks or gratifies the person, our report of his emotion will imply that he is thinking in some manner about the item. If you are curious regarding the purposive behavior to expect from an individual who is undergoing some emotion, and wonder what information will have a calming or aggravating effect upon his state, you will have to discover the object of his emotion. Suppose I know only that my weekend visitor is disgusted, but I have no idea that he is disgusted because the kitchen is so messy. Then all I can do is tell some jokes or perhaps offer him a narcotic to cheer him up. But as soon as I learn precisely what is upsetting him, I not only have a more direct method to alter his mood. I can also predict that if I do nothing about the untidiness, he will become increasingly troubled as dishes accumulate, and that in desperation he may clean up the disorder himself. More important than giving me reasons to act, and to predict his intentional behavior, my discovery of the object of his disgust will enable me to interpret his activity by reference to what disgusts him. I will understand why he is sweeping the kitchen floor. He is doing this not merely to distract himself from thoughts about the inclement weather, or so that he will not be bothered by the noisy children. No: the weather and the noise are not what upset him. It is the cluttered kitchen; and he is putting it back in order because it disgusts him. Evidently this story of his emotion entails that he has various thoughts about the object of his emotion.

But we must realize that the event of my guest being upset by the dirty kitchen has many other characteristics. As I remarked, we do not have to report it as a bout of emotion, and consequently as an emotion having such-and-such an object, which will entail that there is thinking on his part about the object. Of course, then we lose the practical, predictive and explanatory benefits I listed. Now these may not interest us—if, for example, we are neurophysiologists. Our goal would then be to describe the event in terms which have no bearing upon *what* disturbs my guest.

This approach circumvents the subsidiary quarrel I mentioned among entailment theorists themselves about whether each form of emotion is logically tied to a particular range of thinking—for instance, remorse to firm belief that you did X and that X was wicked; hope to uncertainty. This becomes a minor problem of interpreting particular emotion terms, and will arise only when we have used such terms to report an event which is an episode of emotion.

(2) WHEN OUR EMOTION IS BASED ON FALSE BELIEFS, IS IT
FALSE?

For historical reasons, however, one species of emotion is
worth investigating further. This will be my second conun-
drum about the relation between our emotional attitudes
and the cognitive capers on which they are based. Plato's
discussions of pleasure are responsible for my interest. I
understand the term 'pleasure' broadly, so that it may
encompass one's delight that Billy received a scholarship;
one's satisfaction at the defeat of a racist Congressman;
one's enjoyment of a tennis-match, *qua* observer or
player; perhaps even one's relief upon learning that a
friend's tumor is benign. Pleasure can be calm or
vehement. It can be directed toward particular things, or
general conditions like rising employment. Its objects may
be past, present or future; and they may be specified by
propositional 'that'-clauses, by direct-object phrases or
indirect-object phrases. Accordingly, what sort of thing
pleases you will vary. You may take pleasure in events,
merely because they have occurred, are occurring or will
occur. Your pleasure may be in bringing about such
events, or in performing actions to which the events
correspond. Finally, perhaps you simply enjoy a material
item—without being pleased that you own it, being
pleased that it exists, or even taking pleasure in con-
templating it. With this broad interpretation, is there
anything I want to exclude? Yes, for purposes of this
inquiry regarding pleasure and belief, I mainly want to
neglect very general pro-feelings such as contentment and
happiness, which have no more definite object than 'one's
life'—or even worse, 'the order of things'. I have no
analysis for clearly objectless forms of pleasure: feeling on

top of the world, euphoric rapture and ecstasy. These emotions need have no cognitive element.

As I said, Plato originated the riddle about pleasure and thought which concerns me. In an important passage (36-44A) of his late dialogue *Philebus*, he has Socrates argue at length that if your pleasure is based upon an erroneous belief, then your pleasure as well as your belief is false. Plato's doctrine, and the most natural objection to it, stand out in the following exchange between Socrates and his respondent Protarchus:

> S: I fancy we often experience pleasure in association with an opinion that is not right, but false.
>
> P: Of course, and then, that being so, Socrates, we call the opinion false, but the pleasure itself nobody could ever term false (37E, Hackforth translation).

I do not want to indulge in exegesis. Still one point must be made clear. Socrates is not saying it is false that you believe you will inherit "great quantities of gold", or false that you are delighted at the prospect of such wealth. Someone whose pleasure is false, according to Socrates, "always really feels that pleasure, yet sometimes it has no reference to any present or past fact, while in many cases, perhaps in most, it has reference to what never will be a fact" (40D). To neutralize the objection from ordinary language, that "the pleasure itself nobody could ever term false", we only have to recall the parallel cases where we do talk of 'false hopes' and 'false fears'.

But are worries and hopes which are grounded on mistaken hunches and convictions literally false? What strongly inclines me to say so, and to take a similar view of analogous specimens of pleasure, is the difficulty of detaching the so-called "pleasure itself" from its cognitive underpinning. As we have just seen, it does not seem logically possible for a person to have an emotion regarding O unless he thinks in some way about O. If you stop him from thinking of O, what you have left will not amount to emotion regarding O. You will have bodily agitation, adrenalin flow, facial expressions, blushing or paling. However, these remaining processes have no "reference" to O; one does not tremble 'that O' or 'about O'. To blush *over an agreable compliment* is surely to be aware of the compliment, in the same way that chuckling at a joke depends upon one's having understood or misunderstood—and so having thought about—the joke.

I daresay that the 'What is left over?' argument for not sundering "the pleasure itself" from its cognitive foundations will even have some validity from a neurophysiological standpoint. Suppose that experimenters learn to 'decode' electro-chemical happenings within the brain of someone who is pleased. The experimenters can tell what exactly pleases the man. In this sense, they can say that his neural processes are directed toward an object while he is in a state of pleasure. But must the experimenters not also take it for granted that brain processes are occurring which characterize thought about the same object? Presumably they will declare their subject is both thinking and experiencing pleasure about a single item. I would then challenge them to bring the neural thought-process to an end without terminating the hedonic process which has reference to the object. Whatever neural goings-on are essential to pleasure *about O*, can you find them without neural happenings which figure in thinking about O? In my own 'component' terminology, if a neural element always as a matter of fact turns up when someone is pleased about O, it will have all the characteristics of a neural element which figures in the person's merely thinking of O. In other words, the neural happenings which occur when we are in an emotional state may have peculiarities of their own. For example, they may release adrenalin. But surely they also have features of a brain process which occurs when we merely think, without emotion, of the same object. What is more, I suspect that this would be a matter of definition for my imaginary neurophysiologists. I do not see how they could decide that some cerebral process has to do with emotion about O, and deny that it is connected with any concurrent thinking of his about O.

So much for my disinclination to agree with Protarchus that only the belief on which our pleasure is based can be false, not "the pleasure itself". But my component approach will enable us to avoid strange talk of "the pleasure itself", so that we need not assume the separability of emotion and its cognitive foundation; and yet it will enable us to say that only the belief is false. How does this work? Falsity is confined to the cognitive ingredient of one's pleasure. Falsity is not like a virus, which spreads contagiously from one part of an organism to the whole. Error is not the right sort of thing to be infectuous. Why not? This could set off disputes about what it is for beliefs to be true or false. My component approach offers no special answers to problems of truth as correspondence, coherence or 'endorsement'. But my guess would be that a man's opinion is false when it is related in a different way than a true opinion to items and events around him. This is deliberately vague. But the point is that falsity is a relational feature of one's belief. Relational features are not infectuous. They do not spread from part to whole. My example from chapter 1 of the ghetto uprising, and the constituent acts of its participants, will serve here again. Sam's act of forcing open the door of the grocery may be hesitant and furtive, but the uprising does not—perhaps cannot be said to—have these qualities. By analogy, although my pleasure has belief-constituents which are false , we can deny that it is false—and even deny that falsehood is meaningfully predicable of it. Thus we forego the dubious move of separating my pleasure from the erroneous opinion on which it is grounded, and also avoid the heroic conclusion that pleasure can be false.

3. Are Reasons We Act on Causally or Logically Connected with our Deeds?

Now I approach a debate that is presently more heated than those on emotion and thought and false pleasures. Also more has been written about the puzzling relation between our deeds and the reasons for which we perform them. But the same doctrinal battle-lines are drawn. Partisans of causal analysis maintain that the reasons we act on produce our deeds, while entailment theorists discern logical connections here.* Another overlap should be noted with our general problem about emotions and the thinking on which they are based. Both our emotional

---

* There are other accounts, especially of action, such as R. S. Peters' "rule-following model" in *The Concept of Motivation* [1958]. For simplicity I neglect these analyses. They coincide with what I call 'entailment' theories inasmuch as they dismiss the possibility of causal relations between one's deed and one's reasons for acting.

The following opponents of causal analysis seem to hold theories of either mutual or one-way entailment between action and reasons for action: Foot [1957], esp. p. 75ff; Melden [1961]; Kenny [1963]; C. Taylor [1964], esp. pp. 33f, 42-7, 219, 224-8; R. Taylor [1966], pp. 199, 223; Malcolm [1968], pp. 49ff, 55, 61f, 64. Stoutland [1970], while not accepting an entailment view, rejects causal interpretations and proposes a "telelogical" alternative to them.

Davidson [1963] provides ammunition for counterattacks on behalf of causality. See also Armstrong's systematic development of causal views, in [1968], especially pp. 132-62. Further clarification may be found in Davidson [1971] and [1972].

attitudes and their cognitive foundation-stones may turn up among the reasons why we perform some action, so that we may be said to act on the basis of various emotions and beliefs. Naturally a good number of these beliefs originate in our perception of the objects and events which they are 'about'. Here is an example: A skilled counterfeiter tears to pieces some brand new bills. Why? Because he is annoyed—and obviously convinced by looking—that the ink on them smears. There are other cases where one acts because of a pleasure which depends upon one's erroneous belief. For instance, I enthusiastically inspect and try out a used motorcycle. I am delighted that it is in such fine condition, and purchase it. A day or so later I discover my mistake, and my elation diminishes.

More commonly, however, what we do is said to have its source in our conative, rather than our affective attitudes. But of course our desires and decisions must be based on our beliefs and conjectures in the same sense that our emotions have a cognitive basis. We must at least be thinking of the type of action which we want to carry out. In other respects, we do not find as close a match between what a person thinks and his 'drive states'. Conative attitudes 'that H' are exceptional. What would it mean to declare: 'Max wants (yearns, desires, has the purpose) that he will visit the countryside this weekend'? Yet emotion terms such as 'is delighted', 'is sorry' and 'hopes' fit comfortably before this propositional clause. Now it is true that we can talk of a person deciding or intending that he will visit the countryside; but it would be more natural if we said he decided or intended *to* visit the countryside. Aside from this grammatical gap between conation and cognition, we should notice that it is no easy task to say what a particular desire-specification entails about the agent's thinking. Evidently we can tell in an *ad hoc* manner, as long as we are dealing with familiar cases. But when we consider unusual examples, these entailments are uncertain. Imagine a jaded sportsman who is determined to ski on Mars next Christmas vacation. Given this description of his goal, what beliefs must we attribute to him? Must he think it is more likely than not that he will reach Mars by then? Must he consider the journey technically feasible? Physically possible? What information—or misinformation—must he have concerning the planet? About all we can be sure of is that he has thoughts of skiing on Mars.

I attach less significance to this 'loose' connection between our drives and our thoughts than to the gulf dividing all such mental states from our overt deeds. A causal theorist will quite properly emphasize this gulf. He will ask: "Isn't there a vast difference between wanting, however resolutely, to act, and going ahead? What else but causality can take us from planning to action?" In terms of explaining people's behavior, the causationist will say: "When you account for someone's conduct by reference to various grounds he had at the time, what else can you be offering but a causal explanation?"

In this debate, then, entailment theorists will have to argue pretty resourcefully if they are going to convince us that there is a *prima facie* case for their sort of analysis of actions and reasons. I'll cover only two of their most striking contentions.

(a) The 'Bodily Motion' Argument. This one starts on the action side of the gulf. What do we find there? A mere bodily motion—any physiological change or stasis—by itself will never rank as an action. For example, when your first clenches, we do not always have an instance of you clenching your fist; although we could not have the latter without the former. What must be added to bodily motion? To qualify even as a rote gesture, as something you do automatically or absent-mindedly, perhaps unwittingly and unintentionally, the movement of your body will have to meet a pair of conditions:

(i) It must occur while you are conscious. I take this to mean that you must have *some* fairly correct beliefs about your general circumstances at the time. Negatively speaking, the bodily motion cannot occur while you are sound asleep, comatose, in a fugue state or catatonic trance, if it is to count as something you do. Borderline situations would be if you were heavily drugged, in a deep hypnotic trance, or running amok when your fist clenches.

(ii) Another requirement is that you have at least a moderate degree of control over the bodily motion at the time. You do not have to *be* controlling it; but you must be able, at the time, *directly* to initiate and to inhibit such motions of your body. This stipulation is vague. But we plainly rule out cases where your hand is temporarily or permanently paralysed, and clenches because of some neural spasm, or because you press it against the wall until it closes.

However imprecise they are, conditions (i) and (ii) seem to be entailed by the statement that you perform the action of clenching your fist. For that matter, (ii) entails (i), since a person who is in control of his limbs must be conscious at the time he is in control. Another advantage of requirements (i) and (ii) is that they coincide with our pre-analytical intuitions. We feel that when someone only manages to bring about a particular movement of his own body indirectly—for example when he makes his heart pump faster by running upstairs—that pumping movement is not his action. (i) and (ii) also make sense of our intuitive distinction between verbs of action and verbs which take the active voice but stand for mere bodily happenings. Thus, with the exception of skilled yogins, when people sneeze, digest their food, grow, perspire, bleed, faint or snore, we would deny that their bodily motions can amount to actions. And sure enough, each of these bodily motions fails to satisfy one or both of the foregoing requirements.

The upshot of this 'Bodily Motion' argument is that we conceive of action in general as done by agents with some correct beliefs, and some mastery over their bodily motions. If you report that someone performed even a minimal 'automatic' action, we are deductively entitled to these inferences. Entailment theorists next try to connect up specific actions with specific reasons.

(b) The 'Identification' Argument. Instead of border-line actions like fidgeting and automatic fist-clenching, look at forms of 'higher' or 'purposive' behavior. The argument now is that you cannot identify what type of purposive behavior is occurring unless you explicitly or implicitly attribute definite reasons to the agent. This is supposed to establish a logical connection between action-types and states of mind.

We can skip the trivial cases where an agent is *reported* to have done something on purpose. deliberately, knowingly, or under the erroneous impression that such-and-such was true. Reports of this type do not spell out all the agent's reasons, but they entail that he had some—for example a goal. The same holds when someone is described as performing a task gladly, angrily, enthusiastically, unwillingly, conscientiously, obediently or impulsively. We can deduce, for example, that he was pleased to do the job, and this implies that he had some correct beliefs about his current situation.

What about cases where purpose is denied, such as 'Charles knocked over a lamp unintentionally—it was an accident'? We cannot infer that the agent realized he was upsetting the lamp, or had any goal in doing so. Perhaps he made a random gesture. But then we go back to the previous argument: he must have been conscious and generally in control of such gestures. If Charles faints and his body topples against the lamp, it would not be true to declare that he knocked over the lamp—even 'inadvertantly'.

Turning to undeniable verbs of action, we notice that many of them imply either awareness or intention—or both—on the agent's part. Specimens would be: 'Jane promised to buy groceries; she telephoned the market, and learned that it was still open; she hurried there, selected what she wanted, and paid for everything by writing a check.' Other agency verbs may lack these precise implications, but always entail some beliefs and mastery. Moreover, when using these verbs we can add that the agent's performance was successful or defective, and this implies again that he had specific reasons.

I'll give a lengthy illustration of this entailment, because there are multiple dimensions of success and failure in what we do. The basic story will be that two gangsters enter a billiard parlor where Butch hangs out. Both point revolvers in the direction of Butch. They fire several times. Half a dozen bullets strike Butch, and he collapses.

None of these verbs imply anything about the mobsters' reasons. But the situation alters if we attribute success or failure to our gunmen. If we report that they succeeded in entering his hangout, and in shooting him, we imply that they meant to do these things, and that they were after Butch in particular. Now if it was their mission only to give him a scare this time, by firing over his head, we must

revise our account. We will say they bungled. Another
dimension of success and failure concerns more or less
distant effects. For instance, if Butch is wounded and sur-
vives, we could state either that the gunmen failed to kill
him, or that they succeeded in wounding him. It's obvious
what each phrase entails about their reasons. Looking
further ahead, we can say they were successful or
unsuccessful in frightening Butch's gang out of the
neighborhood. Either way we imply that the gunmen
believed him to be a member of some rival syndicate, and
that their goal in attacking him was to scare his cohorts.
Another perspective we could take has to do with the *kind*
of action they intended to perform, rather than the results
they sought. If they were engaged in a vendetta with
Butch's gang, we might say that they succeeded in striking
back. Had they not attacked, they would have failed to
respond. Again, whether we ascribe success or failure to
them, we imply that they believed the other mob to have
committed some aggression against theirs, and that they
feel obliged to reciprocate. Our overall conclusion is that
you cannot identify any of these forms of success and
failure in action unless you attribute various reasons to the
agent.

That should suffice for the 'Identification' argument.
Together with the 'Bodily Motion' argument, does it
establish logical ties between our deeds and our mental
states? Must causal theorists abandon the field? Not quite.
In conformity with our approach to the general dispute
regarding emotion and thought, we should concede this
much to entailment theorists: They have proven that if you
describe some event as any type of action—minimal or
purposive—your description entails something about the
agent's state of mind, as well as his powers. The bond here
is entirely conceptual, however. In terms of our 'cause'-
'constituent' dichotomy, the entailment theorist has

shown that occurrences must have various mental components in order to satisfy our concept of action. There is no bond, logical or otherwise, between the total concrete occurrence and its mental constituent. Still, this puts a limitation on causal theorists. They cannot initially describe an event as an action, and then say that it resulted from the agent's reasons. They must characterize the event by reference to one of its other constituents—for example as a series of muscular and skeletal changes. Then they can find out whether these ingredient occurrences resulted from the agent's attitudes or their cerebral counterparts. A causal theorist may still emphasize mental constituents of action because they influence so many other processes that figure in the total event. And as we shall notice in the next chapter, nothing we've said bars a causal theorist from establishing that our actions, including their mental components, result from 'external' non-ingredient occurrences.

Perhaps my analysis will be challenged because, underneath its new terminological clothing, it looks suspiciously like a primitive doctrine which Gilbert Ryle and others have refuted. I'm alluding to the traditional view that our deeds consist of bodily motions plus mysterious acts of will, by means of which we bring about the bodily motions. All my analysis shares with this quaint doctrine is reference to corporeal movements, which I shall analyse shortly. On the 'mental' side, I don't say that we perform acts of volition. While I certainly rank our decisions, intentions and desires among the ingredients of actions we perform, it would be a fallacy of division of you infer from this that I believe we 'perform' these ingredients as well. Why should elements of what we do be further deeds? The notes which make up a tune aren't further tunes.

Another point of dissimilarity between my analysis and

the traditional view is this. Suppose that we do after all execute acts of believing and desiring, and these make our limbs move. From this I would never deduce the implausible conclusion that we perform these volitional capers as a means of bringing about their physiological effects—or any effects for that matter. What would it mean to say, 'George is deciding to sit down in order to bring about various contractions of his muscles'? The action we decide to perform may be a means to something else. Our decision is not: it just happens to be followed by further events like muscle contractions.

Since we are talking about these physiological goings on, we might as well turn to our next riddles.

4. Some Mysteries About the Material Elements of Action

(1) IS CORPOREAL MOVEMENT ALL THERE IS TO ACTION?

We can withdraw from the struggle between causal and entailment theorists, although questions regarding causality will continue to preoccupy us. As a change of pace, and ultimately in order to deepen our understanding of action, I turn away from direct examination of its mental ingredients, and attend to its straightforwardly material elements. I start with large scale motions of an agent's limbs. It would be a natural corollary of my analysis so far to hold that our typical deeds comprise a bodily event. 'Typical' allows for the possibility that there are also 'purely mental' capers—for example, a woman's silently resolving to seek a divorce. For such purely mental acts I have no component analysis to offer; but fortunately none of the puzzles in response to which I have developed my analysis require that I elucidate these acts. Thus I shall dodge questions about whether our internal performances must be totally incorporeal in nature, or whether they have some physical dimensions.

My first and last thought-problems in this chapter involve the assumption that our deeds are nothing but bodily movements. In between, I examine an argument to exactly the opposite effect: that corporeal goings-on which accompany action bear no interesting relationship to what we do. Evidently both these mutually incompatible doctrines stand in the way of saying that bodily motion is an element of action.

Before we look at the first enigma, we might ask why so many philosophers take it for granted that actions and bodily movements are identical. I have run across few explicit rationales for this assumption; but it seems to me a plausible inference from the doctrine of causal theorists which we examined in the previous chapter, namely that the reasons on which one acts must bring about one's deed. If you also believe—and I do—that an effect must be distinguishable from whatever produced it, then you must sunder an action from those mental antecedents you think caused it. What is left over but bodily goings-on to identify with actions?

More of that shortly. Three preliminary clarifications may help us deal with the notion of 'bodily movement' which most action theorists have adopted. One point should have been fairly evident, from my discussion of the 'Bodily Motion' Argument in the preceding chapter: philosophers have a rather elastic concept, which allows them to rank "standing fast" (Davidson [1971], p. 11), and "stillness" of one's body (Honderich [1972], p. 187), among corporeal movements. As I interpret this philosophical usage, we can say that a body or a part of it 'moved', although it did not change location, or alter in any non-spatial respect. So motion no longer contrasts with motionlessness.

A second point, worth noticing in connection with my final puzzle in this chapter, is that while action theorists regard our brain as part of our body, they implicitly distinguish cerebral from corporeal events when they talk of one causing the other.

My third clarification is more vital. When most philosophers of action report someone's bodily motion, often they mean only that the person's body, or part of it, figured in a particular event, process or state. But the noun 'movement', in its ordinary and its action-theoretic usage, is ambiguous. For in reporting movement of the person's body, you could mean that *he* moved it. We might call this last a 'transitive' or 'active' sense of 'move' and 'movement'.

Perhaps I should illustrate this abiguity of our key verb and noun. Imagine that Harold is lying comatose on a hospital bed. Of course we could already assert that movement of his body is occurring, in the broad action-theoretical usage of 'movement'. After all, his body is still. Yet he is not holding his body still; so there is no bodily movement in the 'active' or 'transitive' sense. To make this very plain, suppose that a careless hospital attendant rams the electric lunch wagon into Harold's bed, overturning it. Harold's body plummets to the floor. In the ordinary, unelastic sense, we can say that his body moved. But since he did not move his limbs, we would not say that movement, in the 'active' or 'transitive' sense, has occurred. I belabor this latter distinction because particularly in Davidson's ground-breaking essays on action I am often unsure what is meant by 'bodily movement'. Take Davidson's masterful paper in which appears the famous *dictum*: "Actions are mere movements of the body—these are all the actions there are" ([1971], p. 23; see pp. 11, 14, 16ff, 24f). How seriously do we react to "mere"? Should we argue that actions do not belong in the same conceptual basket as the fall of an unconscious person's body? Or, supposing that Davidson includes cases of someone 'actively' moving his limbs among "the actions there are", should we feel challenged to demonstrate that people do more than move their limbs—that they also influence and shape events beyond their epidermis? This latter challenge, incidentally, will bulk large in chapter 5. At present I only wish to call attention to the ambiguity of our key term, 'bodily movement'.

Now we are sufficiently forewarned to confront our first puzzle, Chisholm noticed it a decade ago (see his [1964], p. 616; also [1966], p. 30). But I consider Davidson's formulation of it because Davidson regards it as a central and "insurmountable" problem for causal theorists like himself ([1972], p. 153). In the essay I want to examine now, Davidson seems to equate actions with bodily movements, in our 'active' or 'transitive' sense. He also contrasts action with "the effect caused by my action", baptizing the latter as "the *completion* of the action" (*Ibid.*, p. 145). He would like to spell out an analysis of intentional action in which it is "defined by its causes" (p. 149). These would be "states or events which are causal conditions of intentional actions":

> The most eligible . . . are the beliefs and desires of an agent that *rationalize* an action, in the sense that their propositional expressions put the action in a favorable light, provide an account of the reasons the agent had in acting, and allow us to reconstruct the intention with which he acted (p. 147).

In other words, when someone performs an action of type x, his action is intentional—that is, he x's intentionally—if his action resulted from appropriate beliefs and desires.

Davidson's problem, however, is that "wanting to do something of type x may cause someone to do something of type x, and yet the causal chain may operate in such a manner that the act is not intentional"—by our pre-analytic criteria (p. 152). For one thing, "quaint *external* causal chains" may lead from wanting to a "wanted effect" of one's action (bodily movement), and yet we would have to deny that "the wanted effect was intentional" (p. 152). Davidson's first counterexample to a causal analysis features an armed man who has resolved

to do away with a particular person. The gunman care-
fully fires at his victim. His shots miss. But, unknown to
the sniper, a herd of wild pigs is nearby, and stampedes as
a result of the noise, providentially trampling the victim to
death (p. 152).

Should we agree with Davidson that the sniper has not
killed intentionally, while supposing that he has satisfied
the causal analysis by producing effects which he desires
and expects? I am uncertain. Insofar as this form of
death, and its curious origin, does not appear to us to be
intended, perhaps we should also deny that the final events
here were "wanted". Thus Davidson's first counterexample is not decisive.

His second case is more interesting, for our purposes,
because it has to do with bodily movements rather than
their effects. This time we imagine a mountain climber,
whose hands are clasping a rope. At the other end his
partner dangles helplessly. Now our alpinist is tormented
by an urge to relax his grip on the cord. He also has
appropriate thoughts about what misfortunes will ensue if
he does this. The trick, in Davidson's story, is that our
mountaineer's "belief and want so unnerve him as to
cause him to loosen his hold" (p. 153; see p. 154). Here we
seem to be faced with a "non-standard or lunatic
internal" nexus between reasons for an act of type x, and
an act of type x, which fails to make the resulting act
intentional.

Is Davidson's lunatic internal chain example sufficiently
clear to refute a causal analysis of intentional behavior?
Again I am hesitant. To begin with, we should hear more
of the alpinist's "want". How dominant and settled was
it? For example, did it prevail over the climber's other
competing desires? Did he want to let go of the rope more
than he wanted to continue holding it? More crucially,
was his want equivalent to a decision? This question

creates a dilemma for Davidson's example. If the mountaineer's want was equivalent to a decision that he would relax his grip, then why does Davidson rank the upshot as less than an intentional performance? If this was the climber's own design, how could it "unnerve" him? On the other side, suppose that he has not made up his mind. He only feels like relaxing his grip, but has not given in to his inclination. In this case, ought we to agree with Davidson that the "causal conditions of intentional actions" obtain? In other words, should we expect even a feeble urge for x-ing to cause a man to go ahead and x? I doubt it. So, depending upon how much or how little we equate the climber's want with a resolution, either we conclude that his ensuing bodily movement may not be an intentional performance after all; or else we deny that a causal analyst is committed to supposing that the want produced suitable 'transitive' relaxing motions.

We should also hear more about these motions. Exactly how did things look when the alpinist's "wanting to loosen his hold caused him to loosen his hold"? (p. 154). Once more we seem to face a dilemma. Was his movement deft, careful, perhaps graceful? Then it seems to qualify as intentional. Or was it more like a twitch, a spasm of fatigue? My point now is that if his fingers just 'gave out' from the strain, then this does not sound like the kind of 'transitive' movement that a causal analyst would expect "wanting" to generate. More dogmatically: this spasmodic weakening does not appear to be the sort of thing a person can want in the first place. For we tend to think that a person can only want to execute bodily movements which are in his behavioral repertoire—movements over which he normally exercises direct control.

Thus, whether we approach the case from the perspective of the climber's want, or from the standpoint of his movement, we do not seem to have an unimpeachable counter-instance to causal analyses of intentional behavior.

At this juncture you might try modifying Davidson's anecdote. Perhaps the climber simply *hoped* that his fingers would weaken and slide from the cord. This enables us to escape one horn of the foregoing dilemma, because what one hopes for need not be an action—by oneself or anyone else. But then we are menaced by the other horn. Should the mountaineer get what he hopes for—weakening of his fingers—then it will be uncertain whether this result constitutes an action by him, even an unintentional one. Thus the causal theory which Davidson feared he was refuting does not seem to be overturned, for it specified that desire to perform an action of type x should result in an *action* of type x.

Another approach I take toward this 'lunatic internal chain' story parallels my suspicion of the roundabout manner of causing death in Davidson's earlier 'external chain' example. Death in that case did not result from impact of the marksman's bullets, as he planned. Here, similarly, motion of the climber's fingers only occurs thanks to an intervening—and presumably unintended as well as unexpected—affective disturbance on the mountaineer's part. So in this latter case it remains an open question whether the alpinist desired and anticipated that his fingers would weaken as a result of his shame reaction. In other words, this internal chain is doubly peculiar because it contains an extra link, of a kind not usually present when someone carries out an intentional act. Naturally one's bodily movements will be affected in various ways by one's emotional responses to the desires on which one is now acting. If my goal is to seize the rarest slice of Beef Wellington before any of the other guests have a chance, my embarrassment at my own designs could make the motion of my arm unsteady. But in such relatively 'normal' desire-emotion-movement sequences, the very occurrence of the movement is not causally dependent upon one's intervening emotional reaction. Even if I had not felt ashamed at my purpose, I would have moved my arm toward the beef roast. My shame only made my gesture somewhat shaky. But in Davidson's mountaineering tale, the loosening of his protagonist's grip would simply have failed to occur, if the man had not been unnerved at his desire to relax his grip. So along with my misgivings about our alpinist's want and his eventual bodily movement, I have doubts with regard to his mediating affective response. It seems to bear too heavy a dialectical burden in Davidson's second counterexample against causal analyses of intentional behavior.

There is a further methodological lesson to the climbing story. We see how much of its plausibility as a counterexample derives from Davidson's identification of bodily movement generally with what we called bodily movement in the 'active' or 'transitive' sense. Davidson's yarn seemed to represent a case of desire for bodily movement of type x, followed by bodily movement of type x. But as soon as we inquired whether both were instances of 'transitive' movement, we began to realize that it was quite unclear what the mountaineer was up to. So henceforth we should avoid confusing our two senses of 'move' and 'movement'. For my part, when I say that bodily movement is a constituent of action, I have in mind the general sense. If I thought that the action of relaxing one's fingers were an event-component of the mountaineers's action of loosening his hold, evidently my component analysis would be circular. And in reference to the question with which I opened this section, I see a lot more in action than mere corporeal movement.

Davidson's two apparent counterexamples against a causal theory of intentional behavior oblige us to do more than clarify the concept of bodily movement and the relationship of corporeal motion to our deeds. Davidson's cases also force us to draw up criteria for deciding when a reason-to-movement sequence is, or is not, an intentional act. For example, how would a component theorist analyse Davidson's mountaineering anecdote, and explain both why it may have failed to specify an intentional performance, and what other sub-events would have made it one? My reply would be that originally we seem to have this causal chain of sub-events:

(i)   the alpinist's longing to perform the action of relaxing his grip;

(ii) his belief that if he does so, the rope and his partner will fall;

(iii) his paroxysm of guilt in response to his desire and belief;

(iv) the uncontrollable weakening of his fingers.

If instead, (iv'), the relaxing of his fingers, had resulted directly from (i) and (ii), in the absence of (iii), that would be an undeniable case of intentional behavior. Similarly if the climber had begun to feel ashamed *after* (iv'), the relaxing of his grip. It is worth noting, incidentally, that I do not slip into circularity when I replace (iv) by (iv'). The bodily movement reported by Davidson seems too much like twitching, shuddering, tremors and other movements which occur whether or not one wants them. But (iv') is not supposed to be a 'transitive' movement—*viz.*, the action of realxing one's fingers. It is merely supposed to be a movement within the person's repertory, or at least not one that may elude his control. The crucial point, however, is that the alpinist's desire and his total action, of which his desire is a component, mesh in my revised scenario. Sub-events (i), (ii) and (iv') together constitute the action of our climber loosening his grip—a deed of just the sort he wanted to perform. In Davidson's original script, it was unclear whether we had that kind of fit between the climber's desire and the total sequence, because with (iii) and (iv), we were unsure the sequence amounted to an act.

The most important therapeutic insights we have gained so far about the material side of action are that we should make sure that the bodily movement is of the right sort, and that we should not identify this sub-event with the whole deed. The second lesson will be reinforced by the concluding puzzle of this chapter. Now I turn to a challenge from precisely the opposite direction.

(2) ARE BODILY MOVEMENT AND ACTION ENTIRELY DISPARATE?

I have been explaining how a component analysis enables us to avoid crudely identifying deeds and concurrent motions of the agent's body. At present I want to explore a very different issue, which might encourage us to set up an equally simplistic dichotomy between what we do and what happens within the confines of our epidermis. Two undeniable facts are the source of this dichotomizing tendency: (i) For any action you perform, even a rudimentary deed like squinting, you could have carried out an action of that type even though fairly dissimilar movements of your body had occurred; and conversely, (ii) the movement which actually occurred at the time need not have counted as an action of the type that it was. Here is an example of how these facts may impress philosophers of action. Annette Baier asks:

> Are smiles and waves bodily movements . . . ? They

seem distinguishable from bodily movements, since they require more than mere movement, and do not require any particular movement, specified in anatomical and physical ways. A smile is not identical with a facial movement. Stretching one's opened lips to show the dentist one's bite is not smiling . . . [W]aves and smiles, votes, assertions, exercises of rights and the like are to be distinguished from mere bodily movements . . .

In a footnote she offers the further example of doing a push-up. Performing this exercise is distinct from the movements of one's body, "since lifting one's torso by straightening one's arms to extricate one's broken-legged body from a smashed-up car is not doing a push-up" ([1971], p. 166). I realize that Baier may be talking of bodily movement in our 'transitive' sense: a person moving all or part of his body. Nevertheless her reasoning is surely designed to fit cases of a person's body just moving as he carries out an action.

At any rate, arguments of this kind have gained wide circulation (see Hamlyn [1953], pp. 135ff; Peters [1958], p. 12; Melden [1956], pp. 58f, 66, 70, 73, and [1961], pp. 85, 128-31, 183ff, 199ff; Strawson [1963], p. 66; Goldman [1970], pp. 29, 40-48). For ease of reference, call such reasoning 'The Argument from Alternative Realizations'. It illustrates how an action of the same type could have been realized even if your corporeal movements had been different, and how, under dissimilar circumstances, the actual movements of your body would have amounted to an action of some other type. For instance, your lips parted when you smiled. But even if they had not parted, a smile could have occurred. This 'alternative' event would have been the same type of action. The smile-tokens would not be identical, of course, since the one which occurred was a parted-lips instance of smiling, and the 'alternative realization' we imagined was a closed-lip instance of smiling. From the opposite side, when you are in the dentist's chair, we have the same token—that is, the same stretching and parting of your lips—but it is a token of quite a different action, namely letting the dentist examine your bite.

In what respects can this general form of reasoning prove our actions to be "distinguishable from bodily movements"? Will they be totally separate occurrences, perhaps related as effect and cause? If we prevent or overlook the bodily happening, then there is nothing left which might rank as an action. If my lips neither curve upwards, nor remain frozen in that position, then there is no occurrence which might amount to my smile. Similarly if we disregard the motion or stillness of my lips, and look only for some effect of their 'movement'. No effect will qualify as my smiling.

A 'component' approach to this situation would cast the motion or stillness of my lips as part of my smiling—hence not distinguishable in the way that numerically discrete events, particularly cause and effect, are distinguishable. My smiling includes, but does not result from, the movement of my lips. What other event-components make up my smiling? My treatment of earlier riddles will suggest mental goings-on like my suddenly realizing the double-entendre in a limerick someone just recited; my resulting mood of hilarity; as well as brain-processes which cause my lips to curve upwards. All may be further ingredients of the whole event of my smiling. Why should such events take place when I smile? With regard to mental elements, we might say it is logically necessary that events like these occur whenever a person smiles. The brain processes are at most causal components, and therefore not logically necessary, even if they are in fact the same occurrences as some of the mental ingredients of smiling.

In sum, then, my action of smiling is to be distinguished from mere bodily movement like the arching of my lips, in the way that my bicycle is to be distinguished from the tires which are part of it—although not in the way that one tire may be set alongside its mate. My lightweight bicycle could have, or could have had, different wheels. The wheels that in fact belong to it could have been attached to a numerically distinct bicycle—and particularly to a bicycle of a different, heavier type. These wheels are logically necessary parts, even though they are replaceable by others, because one thing we mean when we speak of an operable bicycle is that it has some wheels or other attached to it. By contrast, its gear mechanism is not logically necessary, since we can imagine a bicycle without gears.

Would some analogue to the Argument from Alternative Realizations justify any more radical separation? We might consider dividing act from movement on the basis of remarks like the following by Melden:

> There may be interior bodily occurrences that cause the arm to rise; indeed, if what physiologists tell us is true, this must be granted. But the elevation of the arm—the rising of the arm—is one thing, the doing or the action of raising the arm is something else again . . . ([1961], p. 66)

A component analysis should discourage us from postulating two realms, or even two discrete items in a single domain. Despite their replaceability, the wheels really are parts of my bicycle. So are the gears, although our definition of 'bicycle' may not mention them. In this sense, we cannot speak of parts and whole as "one thing" and "something else", respectively. We could put the two bicycle wheels alongside each other, but we could not thus separate the whole bicycle from one of its wheels. The same holds for what I do and the movement of my body which is part of my action. The Argument from Alternative Realizations only proves that other movements from a certain range could have taken the place of this movement, and that this movement could have figured in an action of some other type. We may readily admit such possibilities without sundering my deed from its bodily-motion component, and especially without retracting our view that the latter really is an ingredient of the former. Finally, although we have to deny that my action and its bodily-motion component are causally interrelated, we may readily admit causal ties among sub-events themselves. For instance, neural and perhaps also mental goings-on affect the large scale movements of our bodies.

I hope that this method of coming to terms with the Argument from Alternative Realizations has dispelled some of the bafflement we may have felt about the relationship between what we do and what our bodies do. I turn next to more specific philosophical quandaries over the material side of what we do.

(3) A RIDDLE ABOUT MUSCULAR CONTRACTIONS

This brings us back to causal theorists, although the difficulty which I consider now is unrelated to their quarrel with entailment analysts. The anomaly they have spotted does not concern action generally; but it takes very definite form in connection with performances where we can distinguish between the agent's main corporeal motion and other goings-on within his body. Here is a stock illustration: When you clench your fist, the principal movement of your body will be the closing of your fingers.

Causal theorists observe, however, that before your fingers draw together, your forearm muscles begin to ripple. Along with this temporal disparity, we cannot help seeing a spatial distinction. And since we observe it to happen that muscular contractions like these are regularly succeeded by the closing of people's fingers, we have all we need for a Humean assertion. Causal theorists like R. M. Chisholm ([1966], pp. 36, 44; [1969], pp. 201f, 216f; [1971], p. 38ff) and Richard Taylor ([1966], pp. 195f), put it as follows: Your action of clenching your fist is an effect of your arm muscles tensing and relaxing.

So far there are no mysteries. But now suppose you learn which muscles tighten and expand when you clench your fist. Then can't you make them do so by closing your fingers? The preposition 'by' is crucial. You cannot simply tense those muscles, 'directly' as it were, without clenching your hand. This latter performance does seem to cause the contractions. If we grant all this, however, we face a dilemma: Either we must deny that 'You make those contractions occur by clenching your fist' means 'You cause them'; or else we must deny the temporal priority of causes over their effects, as well as the asymmetry of causal relations. The priority and asymmetry principles would not hold if we suppose (a) that your subsequent action of fist clenching brought about the earlier event of your forearm muscles contracting, and (b) that these same muscle contractions bring about your fist clenching—which makes the causal relation here symmetrical.

How much would it help if we insinuate to worried causal theorists that they have confused your performance of clenching your fist with its principal bodily-motion component, namely the closing of your fingers? I think they would only reformulate their puzzle in slightly more obscure terminology. They would speak of two events which you bring about, or 'make happen'—one by means of bringing about the other. Perhaps their restatement would go: (a′) At time t_1+n, you bring about the event of your fingers closing at t_1+n, and thereby seem to make an earlier event happen: the rippling of your arm muscles at t_1; moreover, (b′) it still seems to be true that the rippling of your arm muscles causes the closing of your fingers. This restatement does not give us perfect reciprocity of causation, since (a′) specified only that *you*, at $tn+_1$, made an earlier as well as a contemporaneous event take place, while (b′) specifies that the later event which you made happen also resulted from the earlier event. Nevertheless it is sufficiently mystifying to imagine that you can bring about earlier arm muscle contractions, which in turn have already caused the very finger movement which you brought about in order to make them occur!

However that may be, my component approach dissolves the original enigma along with the variant which I devised for causal analysts. We need only reclassify the tensing of your forearm muscles as another bodily motion ingredient of your overall gesture, together with the principal bodily motion component—the closing of your fingers. My therapeutic reminder is that you are a human agent, with control over such parts of your body as your fingers. When you carry out the action of clenching your fist, it doesn't coincidentally happen that your fingers draw together. That would be a kind of miracle, not an instance of someone clenching his fist. Evidently a number of other events take place, between your cerebral cortex and the extremities you move. One intervening occurrence is the tensing of your forearm muscles at t_1. If causal analysts wish, they can say you make this happen; but in return they must allow us to date this 'making happen' at t_1. Admittedly you did not realize at t_1 that you were making this happen. At least so long as you were unaware that your arm muscles ripple just before your fingers close, your intention may have been only to bring about the closing of your fingers. But in fact you also made your arm muscles tense just before. Or if we prefer to drop this phraseology of 'making happen', we can report that you only intended to clench your hand; and furthermore that the principal bodily movement which occurred when you did so was the closing of your fingers. This latter movement resulted from a number of preceding events whose nature you ignored. So although you did not know it, earlier events like the rippling of your arm muscles are also components of your act of fist clenching, and help cause the motion of your fingers.

Whichever way we talk, the contraction of your forearm muscles precedes, and occurs in a distinct region of space from, the resulting motion of your fingers. No doubt they are causally related—but in the standard asymmetrical manner. Presumably the earlier tensing of your arm muscles brings about the closing of your fingers. There are no grounds to assert the converse as well. For imagine that your arm muscles are now contracting, and that your fingers will soon close. How has that future event already produced its effect? Isn't it more likely that previous neural events have done that job? Thus our priority and asymmetry assumptions regarding cause and effect seem to be out of danger. All we have to do is regard the tensing of your arm muscles as an event which helps constitute, rather than cause, your action of fist clenching. This will not put the contractions outside the causal network. They will be effects of preceding neural processes and causes of your fingers' motion.

I believe my component approach does more than neutralize apparent causal anomalies. It gives us a sharper picture of the material side of behavior. A bodily motion component may be described in more minute detail, for example as a muscular contraction. In fact, bodily motions surely are nothing but such goings-on, as well as motions—in the broad sense—of a person's bones and joints. These constituents of bodily motion, and hence of action, we can also report in the yet more refined vocabulary of chemistry or sub-atomic physics, depending upon our interests. On this view, processes in our brain would be motions occurring in one region of our body, which affect and are affected by what happens in other areas. Why set them apart with the label 'brain processes'? The answer might be twofold: Some of these processes may be the same events as our having reasons to act. For another thing, perhaps because we are less informed about them than about the movements of our limbs, bones, joints and muscles, it is usually not one of our intentions when we act that such cerebral events should take place. On this last score, muscle contractions would have border-line status. If I clench my fist intentionally, I must expect and desire some large scale movement of my fingers, and presumably of the appropriate bones. What about tendons in my hand? When we go on to consider my arm muscles, it is even less clear that I intend them to move. Of course it is trivially true that when I deliberately perform an action of some type, I must intend that those events should take place in all regions of my body which are required for that type of action—whatever they are. But a distinction remains: I would just as soon forego everything except the 'central' bodily movement, such as my fingers closing.

Although we achieve these gains in clarity about bodily motion and muscular contractions, we must face two oddities. One is temporal: On my analysis of muscular contractions as elements your fist-clenching, won't it follow that this action begins before your fingers start closing—namely at the moment your arm muscles tense? Yes, we will have to date such actions somewhat earlier.

But ultimately is this any stranger than discovering that a preliminary windup is an integral part of certain baseball pitches? An example from outside the sphere of action would be our discovery that some particular type of illness actually begins with minor disorders, to which we paid no attention, long before the onset of principal symptoms. The second oddity about my component analysis is that I seem to be implying that one thing you do when you clench your fist is to flex your arm muscles. This impression is erroneous. On my interpretation, it is an open empirical question whether you also perform such acts while clenching your fist. My analysis only specifies that, as a matter of fact, such muscular contractions take place—not that your 'perform' them.

This teaser about action and muscular goings-on should be a good warmup for our last mystery concerning physical aspects of behavior.

(4) DOES NEUROPHYSIOLOGY SHOW THAT WE NEVER ACT OF OUR OWN FREE WILL?

We have considered three debates over the material side of action: first a pair dealing with 'bodily' dimensions in general, and then one about the relation of our deeds to the movements of our muscles which occur when we act. Our last puzzle regarding action and the body will be quite different in nature, and will concern events that unfold within the agent's nervous system. As readers can guess, my solution will resemble my treatment of quite different philosophical worries concerning neural processes during perception (chapter 1, section (1)). That is, I shall contend that no problem arises if we regard some concurrent brain processes as neural components of what a person does—which is hardly to say that he also 'does' such brain processes! But before we spell out this kind of approach, we must put ourselves under the spell of a rather widely discussed riddle about what happens inside our cerebral cortex before and during action.

Neurophysiologists have learned that characteristic patterns of electrical activity occur in our brains whenever we engage in supposedly 'voluntary' behavior. For present purposes, it is of no concern what happens when we are subject to coercion, emotional pressure, drugs or hypnosis. Causal theorists are bothered because these findings about voluntary behavior suggest that an observer who knows what is going on in your brain at present can forecast your subsequent deeds. Presumably the cerebral events he is observing now cause your future action. But if it is determined by what has gone on in your cerebral cortex beforehand, how can your future deed be voluntary? How can it be 'up to you' to· perform the action when the time comes? Its cerebral antecedants seem to make your future deed inevitable. Ironically, our scientific search for causes of voluntary behavior leads us to conclude that it isn't voluntary!

Perhaps I should elaborate, and also make it clear that this worry continues to trouble philosophers of action. In a very recent collection of essays to which I alluded in section (1) of this chapter, Professor Ted Honderich reasons as follows. First he assumes that our "brain states" are "effects"—either of earlier and concurrent brain states, or else of "physical" events beyond our nervous system. Secondly he takes it for granted that many brain states are "correlates" of our "experiences", and particularly of such "experiences" as "decidings and choosings". Thirdly, Honderich lays it down that some brain states "are *causes*, both of other states of the brain and also of certain movements of one's body." Then he adds a crucial assumption: "The latter are actions . . . all actions are movements, or of course stillnesses, caused by states of the brain'' ([1972], p. 187; see pp. 189, 199–205, 214). We already noticed difficulties about this postulated reduction of act to bodily movement. But let us see what conclusions Honderich extracts from this reductive assumption and his three main "premises". According to Honderich,

> It follows . . . that on every occasion when we act, we can only act as in fact we do. It follows too that we are not responsible for our actions . . . (p. 187).

> There are . . . uses of 'can' such that it does *not* follow from the premises that one can only act as one does . . . [But] there is one use of 'can' such that it does follow . . .
> The relevant use is bound up with causation, and it is 'cannot,' rather than 'can,' that is of the greater pertinence. To say that something, *A*, cannot happen in a given situation is to say that something else, *not-A*, is caused to happen. To say that something, *B*, can happen . . . is to say that something else, *not-B*, is not caused to happen. (p. 202)

> When we say that a man can do *G* we mean or presuppose, I think, that he is not compelled to do *not-G* and also that he is not caused to do *not-G*. (p. 203)

> [T]he responsibility in question *is* essentially a characterization of something *as* inconsistent with actions being effects. (p. 210)

> To regard a man as responsible for an action . . . *is* to make an assertion of individuality. It is to take the position that the action has not got a general explanation . . . his action *cannot* be explained in such a way that all of its features cited in the explanation are

explanatory in virtue of being instances of a type. (p. 211)

I quote Honderich's statement and solution of this worry about neurophysiology, freedom and responsibility only because of their relatively fresh vintage. There are many other well-known formulations and answers—most of which have come under attack from philosophers who see only a bogus problem here. Although I am unconvinced by Honderich's way of establishing a threat to freedom, and his hint that free actions should only be amenable to "what might be called individual explanation" (p. 211), I shall not attack his or any other writer's treatment. For the component approach which I have been developing circumvents the problem altogether.

If we rank the threatening cerebral events in question as constituents of our voluntary behavior, they could not be causes which somehow make such behavior inevitable and hence unfree. By reference to Honderich's and many other statements of the problem, a component approach is incompatible with Honderich's assumption that "all actions are movements, or . . . stillnesses" of an agent's body. If 'what we do is to result—inevitably—from electrochemical processes within our nervous system, then it must be a separate occurrence. The movement of the rest of our body is easy to distinguish from events in our cerebral cortex and its peripheral extensions. But if we introduce a constituent analysis, our action will encompass both bodily movement and neural processes. The whole action cannot therefore result from one of its ingredient events. Consequently we will be unable to raise the specter of our own brain processes making our actions unfree. It will remain possible, and indeed plausible, to suppose that cerebral event components of our action determine bodily-motion components. But how could that deprive us of freedom? Would we prefer that motions of our bodies should be uncaused, and occur at random; or anyway that no events within our brains should affect happenings elsewhere in our bodies?

I realize that I have only covered the relationship between what goes on now in our brains and the movement of our limbs. But before I explain why the hookup between future action (or bodily movement) and present brain processes is analogous, I want to consider independent justifications for the proposal to regard neural events as constituents of action generally. One rationale appeared already in the previous chapter: These electrochemical happenings may be the same events as our becoming and remaining aware of reasons for what we do. If the reasons we act on are components of our deed, then these brain processes should have the same status.

But even if we ultimately decide that no neural event is identical with the persisting event (or state) of one's having grounds on which he is acting, we still ought to rank his cerebral processes among the ingredients of his deed. This time we can appeal to cybernetics. Physiologists and information theorists have established that in all animals, including humans, many involuntary bodily processes and voluntary actions are controlled by feedback messages to and from the organism's central nervous system. For example, body temperature of warm-blooded animals will stay fairly constant, because whenever such an organism becomes overheated, warning signals flow to its brain from nerve fibers in the proximity of epidermal blood vessels. As a result, other electrical impulses go back to the blood vessels, causing them to dilate. This puts the vessels nearer the air, which cools the blood in them. The same original messages may also cause the brain to send out impulses which activate the animal's sweat glands, and evaporation of sweat will cool the animal. Corresponding processes occur if its body temperature drops. And similar automatic adjustments take place when animals engage in purposive behavior. I reach out for a mug of beer. Information about the movement of my arm and fingers will flow constantly to my brain through nerves in my arm. My eye will send on impulses recording the distance between the beer glass and my hand. Both sets of impulses will cause my brain to transmit messages which regulate the futher motion of my arm and finger muscles. Once there is contact between the beer mug and my hand, impulses will relay this information to my brain, which reacts so that my fingers will continue pressing against the mug handle. Generally, if such automatic negative and positive feeback processes are impeded, our purposive behavior ceases to be coordinated and effective.

How do such considerations from cybernetics make it reasonable for us to see those brain processes which initiate the movement of our limbs as elements of what we do? We can hardly gainsay that feedback processes from muscle to cerebral cortex, and the regulating impulses which result, are part of the overall event which is our action. Moreover, such feedback involves our brain. So why should we not also allow component status to those more central brain events which start everything off?

My proposal will enable us to look at the peeping neurophysiologist in a new way. He watches our brain, and spots happenings there which to him are signs of what we are going to do in the near future. Now suppose that these premonitory happenings are the initial event-components of our deed. Then they cause the forthcoming bodily motion components and regulative feedback components that help fill out our action. So our neurophysiologist is simply predicting from part to whole: he is foretelling what our action will turn out to be, on the strength of observing one of its early event-constituents.

I think we make such forecasts frequently. Here is a parallel case. It is halftime during an American football game. We notice a drum majorette enter the field from a door underneath the grandstand. She is swinging her baton in rhythm. We prophesy that there will be a parade, led by her. And sure enough, a marching band almost immediately follows behind her, and goes through various maneuvers during the next few minutes. In my terminology, the halftime parade consisted of numerous sub-events, among them the entry and subsequent high jinks of the drum majorette who was leading the band. Her behavior was an integral part of the collective performance, since there were obvious causal and conventional relations between what she did and the activity of the musicians under her command. Her action of directing the band had already begun when she preceded it onto the field. Accordingly, the parade, of which her activity was a sub-event, had actually started when we noticed her entering the field. But at that stage not enough sub-events had taken place to justify our claim that we were already observing the parade. Consequently, if anyone said at that juncture that a parade was beginning, there would be a predictive aspect to his statement; for his statement would turn out to be true only if further sub-events occur which, along with the drum majorette's initial antics, collectively constitute a parade. Another point is that once the musicians have marched out and followed her through the pre-arranged maneuvers, you cannot any longer say that the parade and her directional activity are separate occurrences. Her antics from the moment she entered the field were part of the parade, though not part of the activity of the musicians under her command. The parade, however, consisted of what they did, plus what she did in leading them.

By analogy, the initial neural goings-on which our

physiologist observes are not enough to conclusively justify him or anyone else in saying what action is in progress. Nevertheless such cerebral events are part of what the agent is doing, since they touch off the bodily movements which help make up the rest of the agent's deed. Our physiologist is therefore not predicting any action which is separate from the cerebral events he is witnessing. What he is forecasting are, at a minimum, bodily motions which he expects to result from these brain processes. As we remarked, those motions cause feedback to the brain, and are regulated by signals from the brain which result from feedback. So presumably these further neural events will have to occur, as well as appropriate bodily motion, if the agent is to act as our physiologist foresees. But it is harmless to overlook these nuances, and simply declare that the neurophysiologist foresees what our whole action will be on the basis of witnessing its first cerebral constituent.

Here we must deal with the grumble, put aside earlier, that my component analysis only accomodates brain processes which immediately antedate motions of the agent's body. What about those which begin long before his limbs move—those which correspond to his deferred impulses, his resolutions to act later when the opportunity presents itself? Surely I would not want to say, in the light of such cases, that a man begins to act as soon as a brain process occurs from which we can foretell appropriate happenings elsewhere in his body?

By reference to the gangster story I spun in Chapter 3, the present complaint is simple. An omniscient neurophysiologist peeks into the gunmen's crania when they decide to shoot Butch. They believe that Butch is not then present, but that he will be at his favorite hangout several hours later. Having observed the cerebral reflections of these mental states, our neurophysiologist foresees that the mobsters are going to fire at Butch when they corner him. How can the cerebral processes here count as elements of the gangsters' future misdeed?

I agree that the present brain processes are not part of an action which obviously has yet to begin. But I want to know more about the observer's causal hypothesis. Does he suppose that the gunmen's present determination to sheet Butch will suffice? What if their decision slips from their minds before they reach the billiard hall where Butch spends his leisure? Or what if their resolution weakens at the pathetic sight of their intended victim? I just do not see how their initial determination to shoot Butch will be efficacious unless it continues through their opening fusillade. Remember also that it is supposed to cause a voluntary misdeed. But if they begin to fire at Butch without still having the intention or thought of doing so, their behavior would not qualify as voluntary. When I say this, I am not disputing the fact that habitual and rote actions are voluntary even though the agent may not be intent on performing them, or aware that he is. For such cases, the only mental element may be minimal overall consciousness—since a comatose person cannot be said to be executing routine deeds. But in this gangster story we do not have an unthinking habitual action.

I conclude that we should place the gunmen's resolution, as it exists just before and during the fusillade, among the ingredients of their misdeed. This seems to me to insure that the gangsters' antecedent planning is efficacious, and that their attack upon Butch is a voluntary performance. In conformity withour previous reasoning, we deny that the whole episode of gunplay results from their conative attitude. Other constituent events, such as the closing of their trigger fingers, will be effects of their settled intention.

There is still a problem with my account of the

gunmen's initial decision to get Butch at a later time. What causal role does their decision have before they start firing? I just denied that it causes their whole action, and allowed it to determine other constituents of their misdeed only after they begin to act. Is their intent to commit mayhem only window-dressing until the time when they go into action? Surely not. If they do not *remain* decided to attack Butch, their original resolution would be unavailable to serve as constituent of their misdeed and cause of other sub-events. It is vital to our story that the gunmen do more than form an intention of shooting Butch. They must also continue in that state until they corner him. What my analysis suggests, however, is that not all vital factors must be causal factors—at all times. The event of the gunmen making up their minds hours before the shooting is not a constituent of what they eventually do. Nor is their state of intending to shoot Butch—until they meet him and carry out their project.

Other cases will diverge from this pattern. Here is one. A woman feels a tug on her purse, and instinctively struggles with the purse-snatcher for possession of her handbag. While thus resisting, she decides to try out some newly learned karate chops on her attacker, and does so with lethal effect. The woman's decision to use karate is an element in her act of struggling, and a cause of various motions of her body—not to mention bruises suffered by her opponent. Yet her decision was not an antecedant event from which we could have predicted her whole act of resistance. After all, it was the purse-snatcher's attempt which provoked her display of self-defense, and her karate decision only accounted for modifications of technique. Of course you may insist that she must have also decided—very rapidly, perhaps unconsciously—to struggle in the first place, and that this split-second resolution preceded and generated her initial bodily movements. Alternatively, you could maintain that she wasn't acting, only reacting, until she decided. But aren't these arbitrary *a priori* methods of ruling out the possibility that she just found herself engaged in resistance, and then made up her mind to see if karate really worked?

My component analysis will be unaffected however we deal with this karate example. I devised the case mainly to challenge our tacit assumption that conative elements must antedate and produce all the other sub-events which make up what a person does. The example does at least prove that a conative element may occur along the way, as feedback constituents regularly do.

Of my four puzzles about material elements of action, two concerned the movements of our bodies; one had to do with what might be called an element of those bodily movements—namely the contractions of our muscles; and the last focussed on neural ingredients, which mostly have a different location, within our skull and spine, than bodily-motion elements of our deeds. The first riddle seemed to depend upon an identification of bodily motion elements with our whole performance, and by denying this identification we were able to dismiss the riddle. Our second mystery turned upon a diametrically opposed contention, to the effect that our action and the movement of our body are entirely disparate. But the supporting argument did prove that any particular movements which help make up an action need not have occurred. Many others from the same range would have been just as good. But since this particular movement took place, it is a genuine constituent of what we did, and 'logically necessary' in the sense that some movement of that kind has to occur if we are to perform that sort of action.

With regard to the sub-events which engendered our other philosophical worries in this chapter, no current definitions of any type of action makes them logically necessary. But as quite ancient investigators learned, our muscular contractions, for instance, play an indispensable causal role in our purposive behavior. During the past century and a half, scientific study of the nervous system has established that the agent's cortical states, and various automatic feedback mechanisms, are equally vital to what he does. No doubt researchers will soon discover further material ingredients of our deeds.

It must be obvious, too, that all the sub-events I have catalogued so far can be sub-divided in turn. Movements of our bodies evidently consist of muscular contractions and changes in the position of our bones. Consequently there was some harmless redundancy in my original list of material constituents of action. This leads to a related point. You can split up muscular contractions into chemical processes occurring within muscle tissue. On the cerebral side, you can re-specify into electro-magnetic terminology what happens within the agent's cortex. More important, you can altogether discard categories like 'muscular contraction' and 'bran process', and divide human behavior into sub-events upon quite different lines. Perhaps a super-scientist of the future might wish to narrate a tale of gyrating sub-microscopic particles which make up the agent's body and brain. This would still be a tale of physical events which are constituents of the person's behavior.

But suppose the mental-neural 'identity' hypothesis began to seem untenable. This might happen because neurophysiologists simply could not find regular enough correlations between situations where we have settled on reasons to act and situations where a definite type of process occurs in our brain. Then I could no longer suppose that any sub-event I list as a cerebral component of action is in fact a 'reason' component as well. I would have to say that brain processes which spark the movement of our limbs must be separate from the sub-event of our having the reasons on which we are acting. I might assume some kind of 'overdetermination' of our limbs' motion, *if* I wanted to say the motion of our limbs can result from our having reasons to act, as well as from co-existing but non-identical processes in our nervous system. Perhaps I can avoid postulating overdetermination if I imagine that the brain processes themselves result from the agent's having reasons to act. What matters, however, is that even if I give up on mental-neural identity, I have no grounds to retract, or even to question, my empirical claim that some cerebral antecedants and accompaniments of limb motion are part of the total event which is a human action. A person's deed will have the material event-constituents we catalogued, even if we add supposedly non-physical 'reason' ingredients to our list.

5. How Are Basic and Non-basic Actions Related?

(1) PLURALISTS VS. REDUCTIVE UNIFIERS

So far, the philosophically perplexing occurrences I have discussed all found a niche among the sub-events which constitute, respectively, seeing a material object (chapter 1), undergoing an emotion (chapter 2), and acting for a reason (chapters 3 and 4). This time I shall deploy the same component analysis to resolve as deadlocked quarrel about the individuation of so-called 'basic' and non-basic actions, both of which seem unsuited to be parts of anything.

The chief antagonists in the debate over act-individuation I baptize Pluralists and Reductive Unifiers. Goldman ([1970], [1971]) and Davidson ([1963], [1969], especially [1971]), I regard as the leading champions of each outlook. The Pluralist-Reductive Unifier dispute erupts over situations where someone moves all or part of his body. Davidson follows a recent tradition and characterizes such happenings as 'bodily motions' or 'bodily movements'. As we noticed (chapter 4, section (1)), this is a very broad sense of 'move' and 'motion', according to which there is movement even when a person's body, and every part of it, is motionless. We also remarked that this concept of a bodily movement is ambiguous. Davidson seems to mean that an action has occurred, that the person has moved—or kept still—portions of his body, perhaps all of it. This 'transitive' or 'active' reading is the only one that fits Davidson's famous contention that "we never do more than move our bodies" ([1971], p. 23; see pp. 11, 14, 16ff, 20-25)—to which I shall return throughout this chapter. Most other philosophers of action seem to have in mind the event of someone's body moving. This is what 'bodily movement' means when it is equated with 'bodily happening' in the Argument from Alternative Realizations, and when Honderich says that "all actions are movements" of one's body (see sections (2) and (4) of chapter 4).

Luckily this broadness and ambiguity of the concept of bodily movement will not affect the Pluralist-Reductive Unifier dispute, which can flare up if we interpret 'motion' narrowly or elastically, and whether or not we mean that the person has moved his body. Here is a simplified account of the Pluralist-Reductive Unifier debate: Intuitively speaking, a basic action has occurred when the agent moves his body—and sometimes when his body just moves. Our preanalytic notion of 'basic' limits such performances to the confines of one's epidermis. As before, we avoid side issues by leaving it open whether there are any basic performances which comprise no overt bodily goings on—for instance mental antics like silent calculation, and suppressed bouts of rage. If they occur, it is clear that such mental basic deeds cannot involve anything *beyond* the agent's skin.

So far so good. Now the source of disagreement between Pluralists and Reductive Unifiers is the familiar fact that normally when a person thus does something with his body, or carries out a 'basic' action, he also performs a number of 'non-basic' actions, which take in many items external to his body. Random illustrations of this would be: In simply waving my hand, I also wave it above the heads of the crowd. By leaning over from the

waist, I bow to a visiting ambassadress. And naturally
there is the pre-eminent causal situation: By moving my
foot downward, I depress the accelerator of my truck, I
drive faster, and so on. Each of my basic performances
seems to be a 'means' by which I inaugurate various non-
basic ·endeavors. For that matter, my non-basic performances may themselves generate, or amount to,
further non-basic deeds—as when by driving faster I
contravene traffic regulations and overheat the engine of
my truck.

Those philosophers whom I label Pluralists and
Reductive Unifiers, respectively, seem to agree on this pre-
analytic státement of the facts. But they propose quite
divergent metaphysical interpretations of it. A central
question which divides them is fairly straightforward:
When you execute a basic deed, and thereby inaugurate
several non-basic undertakings, how many distinct
particular actions do you perform? Pluralists discern a
whole litter of separate non-basic performances alongside
your basic deed which engendered them. More precisely,
to each non-equivalent specification of what you did
in—or by—carrying out your basic action, there must
correspond a numerically distinct individual non-basic
deed. Reductive Unifiers discern but a single performance;
for they assimilate all your endeavors to those basic movements you make with your body, which are the source of
your various non-basic capers. Reductive Unifiers will
obligingly distinguish between basic and non-basic act-
descriptions, while holding that these are descriptions of
just one entity—the event which is the movement you
make with your body (see Davidson [1971], p. 23). In this
sense, Reductive Unifiers abolish the basic/non-basic *act*
dichotomy.

Thus the dispute between Pluralists and Reductive
Unifiers presents us with a dilemma: Either we make a

person who carries out one basic and several non-basic actions sound very busy, or else we deny that he does anything more than move his body.

I plan to set forth this dialectical impasse in sharper detail, and then develop a component analysis of the sub-events which constitute the basic performance and its non-basic offspring. As before, I hope that a component approach will enable us to slip between the horns. My arguments will make use of earlier chapters. I have already discussed sub-events which are 'mental' and 'material' elements of an action, when I dealt with the relation between acting and reasons for acting (chapter 3), and when I examined puzzles about bodily motions generally, as well as muscular contractions and cerebral happenings (chapter 4).

Here is how my earlier arguments apply to the items under debate between Pluralists and Reductive Unifiers. A basic performance of Mathilda's will, on my view, consist of the following occurrences:

(RFA)   Mathilda's conative, cognitive and affective attitudes, on which she is acting;

(BP)   Events in her cerebral cortex, possibly identical with some included under (RFA), which set off happenings elsewhere in Mathilda's body;

(FP)   Neural feedback processes, no doubt automatic, which regulate non-neural happenings produced by RFA or BP in Mathilda's body;

(BM)   Finally, those non-neural bodily happenings themselves—for instance, contractions of Mathilda's muscles, changes in the position of her bones, and whatever else qualifies for the title of 'bodily movement', in the 'non-transitive' sense of that term.

My account of the non-basic actions which Mathilda thereby inaugurates will simply add on pertinent happenings beyond her epidermis. Her non-basic deeds then consist of elements RFA through BM, plus one or more of the following 'extra-bodily' events:

(RC)   Purely relational consequences—the holding of non-causal and non-conventional relations between RFA, BP, FP or BM and various occurrences outside Mathilda's body;

(E)   Effects, or causal consequences, of RFA, BP, FP or BM upon the course of events in Mathilda's surroundings;

(CC)   Conventional consequences, according to rules which are generally recognized in Mathilda's community, of the events RFA, BP, FP, BM, RC or E.

Thus my inventory would not coincide with Danto's, for example; he would add a 'doing' element to her basic performance, but would exclude RFA from it; and he would make her basic action a component of her non-basic deeds; the only other element he lists for non-basic actions being causal consequences (see his [1973], pp. 7, 28–32, 50–7, 71–7, 104f, 119, 186, 194).

(2) MORE ON RELATIONAL, CAUSAL AND CONVENTIONAL CONSEQUENCES

Before I explain how this scheme resolves the Pluralist-Reductive Unifier dispute, I should discuss briefly each of the non-bodily components RC, E and CC. What sort of kinship do they have to the elements of our basic performances? How do they fuse with the elements of our basic deeds to form non-basic actions?

I start with RC. Intuitively speaking, when Mathilda moves her legs and arms in the right way in the right circumstances, the upshot might be that a particular stream is crossed—perhaps for the first time this summer. For example, she jumps, starting on one bank of the stream and coming to rest on the other. This upshot, the stream's being traversed, is a purely relational consequence of her leap. Her jumping does not cause the stream to be crossed, in the way that my daughter's bouncing up and down on my bed causes the box-springs to give way. One reason is that we can take any event which is the cause of another, and imagine it occurring minus its effect. For instance, we can visualize my daughter bouncing vigorously on my bed and the box-springs remaining intact. But how could Mathilda leap, with the stream underneath her, traveling from one bank to the other, and the stream remain uncrossed? Also, we can say how causes operate to bring about their effects—how my daughter's saltatory motions worked to wear down the box-springs. But there is no analogous 'mechanism' by which Mathilda's leap 'worked' upon the stream so that it became traversed.

This same absence of a causal mechanism will strike us if we turn to conventional consequences. Suppose there is a society in which adult men become knights when the ruler touches their right shoulder with a particular cere-monial sword, as they kneel before the ruler. Now a famous composer, Brown, is on his knees. The Queen approaches with the sword in her hand. She extends her arm. The sword reaches Brown's right shoulder. Would amateur scientists in the audience wonder how the sword operated to transform a commoner into a knight—as they might investigate how some vaccine makes people immune to measles? Obviously not. But there is something more to this situation than mere relations between the Queen's behavior, the sword, and Brown's uncomfortable position. Without a background of commonly accepted customs and rules—rules which specify ceremonial practices, rules which define the legal and social powers of a Queen, rules which set forth what it is to be a knight—it would never be a consequence of these events that Brown is a knight. It is because people accept these conventions that the Queen's gesture has the consequence that Brown is knighted. No rules of this or any similar kind are required for Mathilda's leap to have the consequence that the stream is traversed. When there were only benighted Cro-Magnon men around, streams were crossed if the savages jumped from one bank to another.

Despite these differences, relational, conventional and causal consequences resemble each other in one respect: Intuitively speaking, they 'involve' more items than the agent and his body. The event of the stream's being traversed is a change in the stream, and in that special, limited sense an event which is distinct from Mathilda's leap. Brown's becoming knighted is, in an equally restricted sense, distinguishable from the Queen's gesture. The collapse of my bed is, in a quite ordinary sense, a separate event from my daughter's bouncing, which brought it about. We can make this ordinary sense clear if we recall Hume's teaching that an event like my daughter's bouncing may not be followed by the effect we quite naturally anticipate. We might watch her gleeful high jinks and wonder if the bed will break. But when Mathilda jumps from one bank of the stream to the other, it is unintelligible to ask: 'Do you think her leap worked—that the stream will be crossed?'

We notice the same disparity if we compare effects with conventional consequences. If someone is injected with measles vaccine, he may or may not become immune to measles. Although the vaccine normally causes people to become immune, sometimes it does not work, even when it is administered according to medical rules. But if Brown does not become a knight, there must have been some infringement of regulations or custom. Did the Queen use the wrong sword by mistake? Was Brown's candidacy not approved beforehand by the council of noblemen? Were less than the required number of witnesses on hand? Did Brown kneel down on the wrong knee by mistake? If we do not suspect a slip-up of this kind, we cannot wonder if the ceremony will make him a knight. There is no sense in which the ceremony could be *en règle*, and yet fail to 'work'.

As far as my component analysis of basic and non-basic action goes, what counts is that relational, conventional and causal non-basic performances each have characteristic extra-bodily happenings as ingredients. Besides RFA, BP, FP and BM, Mathilda's non-basic action of jumping over the stream will include a relational consequence of those events, particularly of BM: the stream's being traversed. The Queen's non-basic action of knighting Brown will include the conventional consequence that Brown becomes a nobleman—as well as the sword's motion, which is an effect of her arm motion; the relational consequence that the sword approaches Brown's shoulder; and other extra-bodily events which are too trifling to be catalogued here. My daughter's causal non-basic misdeed of ruining my bed-springs will comprise an effect of her bodily motion: the falling apart of my spring-mattress.

(3) POSSIBLE MISUNDERSTANDINGS

I hope this is a sufficiently precise and graphic account of what I mean by the event-components of basic and correlated non-basic deeds. But I should make it clear that I am *not* assuming or implying various things which many previous writers on basic action have taken for granted. First, I have obviously discarded the obscure but persistent idea that anything basic must be somehow metaphysically simple, non-composite and irreducible. I have not attempted to weave this notion of simplicity into my analysis because I have never come across a cogent explication of it. The putative examples of simple action which I have encountered strike me as vulnerable to one or another kind of segmentation. But this brings out a second point, which should be equally plain. As when I discussed the elements of perceiving and emotion, along with the 'reason' and 'material' constituents of human behavior, what I call ingredients of an occurrence are not homogeneous 'slices' or segments of the occurrence—and conversely. My waving my hand part way through the arc it covers is not an element of my basic action of hand waving; and those events which are elements, such as brain processes, are not themselves hand-wavings. A third, more general, point emerges here. I have avoided saying that any element of a basic or non-basic action is itself something I do. Thus I agree with Danto's view ([1973], p. 74) that events composing a basic action are not further actions. I balk, however, when he says that our non-basic deeds *"contain . . .* as components" the basic actions they spring from ([1973], pp. 29–32, 186). Is a subcommittee itself a member of its parent committee? I would suppose that only sub-committee members can belong. Also I do not follow Danto when he posits a 'doing' relationship between a person and events which make up his action—for instance, when Danto speaks of "the event which is done" ([1973], p. 39; see pp. 7, 57; and [1970], p. 108ff). With regard to any event-component of your performance, possibly it is also something you do. Can't we imagine people with direct control over their brain processes—or magical influence over happenings unconnected with their bodies? I leave this open. But I certainly reject Danto's notion of an "event we might be prepared to call a 'doing' " ([1973], p. 75), which "must be left over when we subtract . . . the event which is done from the doing of the event" (p. 39; see pp. 57, 76f).

So much for Danto, and for the notions I shall introduce to settle the Pluralist-Reductive Unifier quarrel over individuating basic and non-basic actions. Now we must sharpen our awareness of the issues between these metaphysicians.

(4) THE PLURALIST-REDUCTIVE UNIFIER DEBATE AGAIN

A new and painfully detailed political science fiction example will highlight the main problems about individuation in this dispute. Imagine the the Prime Minister of Acirema is in emergency session with members of his National Security Board. They have been alerted that fascist Dauphinia may launch a nuclear attack at any moment. On the Prime Minister's desk is a red buzzer which is connected to the launching mechanisms of a whole fleet of ICBMs (intercontinental ballistic missiles)—all aimed at prime targets in Dauphinia. They will automatically warm up and leave their hardened bases within two hours after the red buzzer is activated. An item of legal background is that Acireman statues forbid the Prime Minister from using the red buzzer to initiate a preemptive nuclear attack without parliamentary approval, and he has not had time to consult parliament. Here is an inventory of what unfolds, beginning at time t_1:

From t_1 through t_4, the Prime Minister has a desire to reassure his fellow National Security Board members (RFA$_1$);

From t_1 through t_4, 'lip' neurons fire in his brain (BP$_1$);

From t_1 through t_4, feedback impulses travel between his brain and lips (FP$_1$);

From t_2 through t_4, his lips part (BM$_1$);

The Prime Minister curls his lips (BA$_1$);

From t_2 through t_4, BM$_1$ affects the visual apparatus of the other National Security Board members (E$_1$);

BM$_1$ is interpreted as a smile and a gesture of reassurance (CC$_1$, CC$_2$);

The Prime Minister grins reassuringly at members of the National Security Board (NBA$_1$);

At t_1, the Prime Minister decides to press the red button immediately with his left index finger (RFA$_2$);

From t_1 through t_4, he believes that pressing the red buzzer will unleash ICBMs, which will cause many deaths; but that this is the only sure way to preserve Acirema from Dauphinian fascism; naturally he also feels strong emotions on these topics (RFA$_2$, RFA$_3$, . . .);

From t_1 through t_4, 'left index finger' neurons fire in his brain, and feedback impulses whiz to and fro between his brain and his left index finger (BP$_2$, FP$_2$);

From t_2 through t_4, his left index finger moves downward (BM$_2$);

He crooks his left index finger (BA$_2$);

At t_3, his left index finger reaches the red buzzer (RC$_1$);

The Prime Minister touches the red buzzer (NBA$_2$);

Between t_3 and t_4, the buzzer moves downward (E$_2$);

The Prime Minister depresses the red button (NBA$_3$);

By t_4, a violation of the 'red buzzer' law has occurred (CC$_3$);

The Prime Minister violates the 'red buzzer' law (NBA_4);

At t_4 plus four hours, the ICBMs blast off (E_3);

At t_4 plus five hours, they raze Dauphinia (E_4);

The Prime Minister destroys Dauphinia (NBA_5).

On my component approach, the Prime Minister's behavior would be divided up as follows:

His basic action of curling his lips (BA_1) consists of RFA_1, BP_1, FP_1 and BM_1;

His conventional non-basic action of smiling reassuringly at the National Security Board members consists of those events, together with E_1, CC_1 and CC_2;

His basic action of bending his left index finger (BA_2) consists of RFA_2, RFA_3 and so on, BP_2, FP_2 and BM_2;

His relational non-basic action of touching the buzzer (NBA_2) consists of those events, plus RC_1;

His causal non-basic action of depressing the buzzer (NBA_3) consists of the foregoing, as well as E_2.

Similar procedures will give us the composition of NBA_4 and NBA_5.

There may be objections against my classifying the Prime Minister's smile as non-basic (NBA_1). My rationale is that grinning *to* or *at* someone appears to be a social transaction. So at the least, this is a relational non-basic action. More important, I think an act of smiling depends upon the existence of norms, fads and background events, in order to be a greeting, an insulting sneer, a signal that one is embarrassed, or—as in the example at hand—a gesture of reassurance. These are some of the interpersonal 'moves' which one's smile can be; and it is plausible to assume that agent and audience must share conventions in order that the curling of his lips will be a smile, and that his smile, in turn, will amount to anything further. I am inclined to think that we mark off certain facial motions as smiles because of the further conventional importance they can assume.

But these refinements are secondary. In connection with the Pluralist-Reductive Unifier debate, what matters about our protagonist's lip-curcling (BA_1) is that it is paradigmatically separate from his finger bending (BA_2). My component analysis would allow you to amalgamate BA_2 with various antecedent preparatory basic actions of the Prime Minister, such as his extending his arm (in the direction of the red buzzer) at t_1-n. You would then have the more comprehensive basic action of his reaching out with his left arm and crooking his left index finger. The only restrictions I place on welding basic actions together is that the items you blend involve just one portion of the agent's body, and that the amalgamated basic actions be spatially and temporally continuous. Negatively: they should not be interrupted by movement-less stretches of time and space. Thus you cannot weld BA_2 and BA_1 into a single basic action, finger-bending-and-lip-curling. If you hanker for some kind of alliance between BA_2 and BA_1, you may establish a further category for 'constellations' of discrete basic performances which are spread out in time or space. Curling one's lip *while* bending one's finger, or vice versa, would be such a constellation of numerically distinct basic actions—simultaneous but involving non-contiguous parts of one's body. Crooking one's finger and *later* curling one's lips would be both temporally and spatially dispersed.

You might raise the side issue, 'What holds a constellation of basic deeds together?' I would look to the agent's reasons—here emotions, beliefs, and desires on which the Prime Minister acts when he simultaneously curls his lips and bends his finger. Because he believes that he is initiating a holocaust to save the free world, he has grounds to reassure his councilors with a smile. If a man performs several basic actions without a common belief, emotion, or goal, then I see no rationale for grouping them into a single constellation. But that is immaterial to our present purposes. What counts is that my component analysis of the basic/non-basic distinction will allow you to amalgamate, subdivide, and constellate some basic acts, while preserving the frontier between basic and non-basic. Most important, only events which occur within the frontiers of one's body will qualify as elements of constellated or single basic deeds. Thus my account of what sub-events constitute a basic action will coincide with our pre-analytic concept of basic actions as somehow limited to one's body.

(5) TEMPORAL BOUNDARIES

I owe further explanation of details. Luckily this will help us appreciate the Pluralist-Reductive Unifier controversy. In my fable, the dating of basic and non-basic performances was not fixed. Thus we might ask: when does the Prime Minister's basic action of crooking his left index finger (BA_2) start? It seems natural enough to specify the time when his finger began moving, t_2. But for reasons I canvassed already in section (4) of the preceding chapter, I clock a basic action from the onset of its initial event-component, which I take to be the brain process that sets off an agent's muscular contractions. So both BA_1 and BA_2 start with BP_1 and BP_2, respectively, at t_1.

Could the non-basic deeds one accomplishes by performing basic actions start later? No individuation theorist has held such a view. Consequently I would specify

t_1 as the temporal origin of NBA_2, our hero's grin. With regard to NBA_3, NBA_4 and especially NBA_5, however, sudden doubts may arise. Surely you cannot start depressing a button (NBA_3) before your finger is in contact with it? And isn't it excessively fanciful to imagine someone having begun to demolish a country (NBA_5) before any destruction has occurred? My answer is that you should consider NBA_3, NBA_4 and NBA_5 as multi-phased accomplishments which culminate, respectively, with the red buzzer moving downwards, a law being broken, and the flattening of Dauphinia. In ordinary language we just happen to designate these actions by their terminal phase alone.

We could raise tricky questions about whether all these basic and non-basic actions go on continuously, without interruption, from t_1 until their last component is over. Suppose the Prime Minister golfs for a couple of hours to kill time between t_4 and t_4 plus five hours. Could we say of him while he strolls and putts, "He is destroying Dauphinia"? Doesn't his doing that interfere with his golfing, and vice versa? Perhaps we can explain that one of his current undertakings, now close to fruition, is a nuclear attack upon Dauphinia. One can be engaged in such a course of action while taking 'time out' for other activities.

What to say as the event-components of BA_2-NBA_5 unfold is relatively uncontroversial. Pluralists and Reductive Unifiers are sufficiently at loggerheads on the preliminary issue of when these actions terminate. Remember that their debate is whether non-basic acts like NBA_2, NBA_3, NBA_4 and NBA_5 must be numerically distinct from each other and from BA_1—presumably in the way this 'finger-crooking' behavior is distinct from BA_1 and NBA_1, our 'smile' sequence.

Pluralists would probably focus on NBA_5, destroying

Dauphinia. Even if we have succeeded in explaining how the Prime Minister can *begin* to perform this non-basic deed long before the missiles fall, could we ever explain how NBA_5 might end before they strike? There is a gap of five hours between the time when his basic action of finger-crooking (BA_2) terminates, and the time when the bombarding of Dauphinia is finished. Because of this disparity in temporal dimensions, aren't we compelled to agree with Pluralists that BA_2 and NBA_5 are separate actions? (See Goldman [1971], p. 767f; Davidson [1971], p. 19.)

I won't give my answer until we survey the contrary view of Reductive Unifiers. *En passant*, I should call attention to the fact that both sides assume, without argument, that you must be either a Pluralist or a Reductive Unifier. For Davidson, the only alternative to saying that non-basic actions are identical with their ancestral basic deed is to say that they are numerically discrete ([1971], pp. 18, 21, 22, 23). The only non-multiplying view Goldman considers is the Davidsonian "identity" position ([1970], ch. I; [1971]). Mrs Thomson is most explicit on this point. Her example is the situation where Sirhan Sirhan assassinated Senator Robert Kennedy by shooting him. She remarks:

> It would certainly be an economy if we could identify the killing with the shooting. Sirhan's shooting of Kennedy was a mad, evil act; Sirhan's killing of Kennedy was a mad, evil act. If we don't identify them, we shall have to say that there were *two* mad evil acts performed by Sirhan that night . . . ([1971], p. 115).

If these are the options, we should see how Reductive Unifiers propose to demonstrate their "identity" claim. To begin with, they challenge our quite "natural" assumption—as Davidson expresses it—"that the action whose mention includes mention of an outcome somehow includes that outcome" ([1971], p. 18). According to Davidson, however, this belief

> springs from a confusion between a feature of the description of the event and a feature of the event itself. The mistake consists in thinking that when the description of an event is made to include reference to a consequence, then the consequence itself is included in the described event (p. 22).

Is there any proof that we are confused over outcomes? I find none. But Reductive Unifiers propose an appealing analysis for non-basic deeds, which seems to lop off outcomes. On this analysis, "to describe an event as a killing is to describe it as an event (here an action) that caused a death" (Davidson [1969], p. 229). It follows that "what we thought was a more attenuated event—the killing—took no more time, and did not differ from" whichever basic action brought about the victim's demise (Davidson [1971], p. 22). In our own political science fiction scenario, then, NBA_5 would be identical with BA_2, which causes E_4. To say that the Prime Minister flattened Dauphinia is to say that he moved his finger, which in the circumstances brought about the destruction of Dauphinia. I think it is worth digressing briefly to see what that philosophical verb of all trades, 'to cause', might mean in such a reductive analysis of non-basic behavior.

(6) WHEN DO OUR BASIC ACTIONS TAKE EFFECT?

Suppose we grant Reductive Unifiers their linguistic

hypothesis—that 'kill' means 'perform a bodily movement which brings about another person's death'. Our problem in section (5) was to decide when non-basic actions like killings are over. So now we must ask this about causing deaths. We might as well put it in terms of the past tense: When is it true to report that the gunman has killed his victim, that the Prime Minister has razed Dauphinia? For the Reductive Unifier, this amounts to asking when it is correct to declare that our protagonists have finished doing whatever causes such-and-such an outcome. But wait: our hard-working verb 'to cause' lacks all indications of tense. Don't we wish to put the whole substitute-sentences in the past tense, like their originals, and say that our protagonists have caused the outcomes isn question? Here we must consult Davidson's most thorough exposition.

As we noted earlier, Davidson first asks us to "interpret the idea of a bodily movement generously . . . enough to encompass such 'movements' as standing fast and mental acts like deciding . . ." ([1971], p. 11). These "movements" he calls our "primitive actions". Next, in order to illustrate "the collapse of all actions into the primitive" (p. 25), he adapts a story from *Hamlet*. The wicked queen holds a vial of poison in her hand. The king sleeps, his ear conveniently exposed. Here are some phrases with which Davidson would allow us to record the queen's behavior:

> "The queen moved her hand" . . . "thus causing the vial to empty into the king's ear" . . . "thus causing the poison to enter the body of the king" . . . "thus causing the king to die" . . . "The queen moved her hand thus causing the death of the king" (p. 22f).

After starting out briskly with the past tense "moved",

we fall into uncertainty with "thus causing". But perhaps there are grounds, not acknowledged by Davidson, to withhold the past tense 'has caused', while asserting that the queen has moved her hand. For investigatory purposes, we should imagine ourselves at the moment when the queen's primitive action of moving her hand is completed. Poison is cascading towards the king's ear, but has not yet reached it. Hence the king is not yet stricken, and his veins are free of poison. Obviously his death has not occurred.

With the poison in midair, should we report that the queen has already caused it to fill his ear, to disturb his vital functions? Has she, or her primitive action, brought about his death? As the question I began this section with may suggest, I doubt whether it is correct to say that all these effects have been produced by this time. And my skepticism is reinforced by a rhetorical flourish of Davidson's. He asks:

> Is it not absurd to suppose that, after the queen has moved her hand in such as way as to cause the king's death, any work remains for her to do or complete? She has done her work; it only remains for the poison to do its ([1971], p. 21).

My misgiving is that if it "remains for the poison" to take effect, we seem forced to deny that it has already caused the king's death. And if the poison has not yet produced this outcome, how can we declare that the queen herself has already caused her husband's death? Thus it appears that although the queen's primitive action is terminated, the non-primitive causings which Davidson attributes to her must be still in progress. So the latter occupy more time—and space as well, no doubt. Accordingly, they cannot be identical with her primitive hand movement.

This reasoning does not hinge on the special character-istics of poison. We speak similarly of other inanimate 'agents'. When we administer smallpox vaccine, we have to wait a day or two for an immune reaction. We only say the vaccine has 'taken' when the reaction becomes manifest. Another medical example would be swallowing aspirin because you are feverish. Your temperature will not begin to drop for at least twenty minutes. Has the aspirin already taken effect? I am reluctant to say that it has already made your fever decline. Likewise with the side-effects of swallowing aspirin: until they occur, we should not say that it has produced them. Admittedly the aspirin and the vaccine—thought not the airborne poison—starts working in some manner right away. But this immediate effect is quite distinct from the long-range outcome—the way we expect it to work.

Evidently we must retract what we said about the Prime Minister's non-basic deeds at the end of section (5). By time t_4, he has bent his left index finger, thus completing BA_2. He has caused E_2, the red buzzer's motion. So he has depressed the buzzer (NBA_3). But he has not caused the ICBMs to blast off; rather, he has done what *will*, four hours hence, cause them to go (E_3), and one hour after that, cause the destruction of Dauphinia (E_4). Thus at t_4, he has not brought about that destruction, and his non-basic action NBA_5 is not terminated.

Reductive Unifiers may react to this in several ways. They might reject my past-tense reading of their causal analysis of non-basic actions, and insist that 'cause' is really a tenseless verb, like the verb 'equal' in mathematical discourse, so that we cannot ask when a basic action has caused its effect. Our reply would be that in civil liability suits, criminal cases, newspaper reports and so forth, 'cause' appears to have tenses.

At this juncture, or perhaps instead of propounding a

tenseless interpretation of 'cause', Reductive Unifiers may proclaim that they are unconcerned with the way lawyers, journalists and other non-scientists use the verb 'cause'. What interests Reductive Unifiers, on this second line of defense, is a rational reconstruction of scientific thinking about events and causal relations between events. Reductive Unifiers want to systematize such thinking, and elucidate its underlying structure. For reasons which we bumpkins are incapable of understanding, Reductive Unifiers deem it more rational either to stipulate that an outcome has been caused by a basic action as soon as the basic action is completed, or else to stipulate that 'cause' will be a tenseless verb in situations where we say a basic action causes some upshot. Either of these stipulatory moves may fill us with awe; but it should be obvious that they are not arguments—only exercises of authority: So far, then, Reductive Unifiers have not vindicated their contention that non-basic actions are identical with the basic performance with engenders them.

(7) THE 'NO FURTHER EFFORT' ARGUMENT—AND BACK TO OUR DILEMMA

Reductive Unifiers may try a third strategy, which impresses me as a very beguiling argument indeed against our dissenting view that a basic action has not caused a result to occur until the result occurs. Taking up our fable again, Reductive Unifiers would remark, quite correctly, that after t_4 nothing is left for the Prime Minister to do. His work is complete. Without further intervention by him, totalitarian Dauphinia will be flattened in a matter of hours (see Davidson [1971], p. 21f; Thomson [1971], pp. 115, 119, 121, 127). The Prime Minister might keep his fingers crossed during the interval, but such behavior contributes nought, causally speaking, to the end-result. Similarly if he checks constantly on the progress of his ICBMs. As long as no further activity on his part is causally required, once he has executed the fateful movement of his left index, we seem to have every reason to assert at t_4 that he has brought about the ruin of Dauphinia—which *ex hypothesi* means that he has destroyed it.

Of course we cannot know for certain at t_4 that the destruction has been caused. But is that relevant? Many reports of past happenings are true although we cannot establish, at the time of utterance, that they are true. A seeming disanalogy is that with standard past-tense statements, nothing that happens now can possibly interfere with the past event in question. Does this hold for the statement, made at t_4, that the Prime Minister has already destroyed Dauphinia? It is possible, logically and 'physically', that events between t_4 and t_4-plus-five-hours should impede the destruction. That is, some type of interference *could* occur. But, Reductive Unifiers are sure to reply, nothing will in fact prevent the holocaust. It is already determined at t_4.

This dialectic could go on. Moreover, we seem forced, by temporal considerations here, to accept either the Pluralist's view that BA_2 and its non-basic progeny are all separate deeds, or the Reductive Unifier's counter-intuitive reading of tensed non-basic action statements.

Is the dilemma irresistable? Take the first horn: Have Pluralists furnished us any proof that NBA_5, destroying Dauphinia, is a supplementary deed by the Prime Minister, alongside his basic action of crooking his finger? Reductive Unifiers are surely right this far: he goes through no further exertions. All we should concede to Pluralists is that when he razes Dauphinia, he accomplishes more—not that he does something extra, such as smiling in addition to crooking his finger. What more does he accomplish? Thanks to the circumstances and surroundings in which he bends his finger, this basic action results in the devastation of Dauphinia (E_4). Such intended consequences, along with unforeseen ones for which a law court may impose liability, or any other results that a commentator thinks noteworthy, may all rank as things the Prime Minister accomplished by crooking his finger. Consequences are thus elements of what he non-basically accomplished. Hence it is correct to report that he carried out BA_2 *and* that he carried out NBA_5. But this conjunctive statement does not record distinct, separate feats, in the sense that his finger-crooking (BA_2) is distinct and separate from his lip-curling (BA_1).

The other horn of our apparent dilemma was that we may have to compress NBA_5 into BA_2. We need not accept this upshot either. We can admit that the Prime Minister's non-basic accomplishments, like NBA_5, have more extensive spatio-temporal dimensions than his basic performance which is their fountainhead. But to recognize the broader frontiers of NBA_5 is not to recognize a supplementary deed alongside BA_2. The USSR takes in considerably more territory than the Socialist Republic of Great Russia, but these are not separate states alongside each other, either geographically or politically. Moscow is the capital of both; many officials have posts in the governments of both; and all Great Russian citizens are citizens of the USSR.

There are less literal but equally unproblematical analogues for such a basic/non-basic act relationship. Jane pierces her right ear lobe for a new earring. She thereby pierces her right ear. How many parts of her anatomy has she pierced? If we recognize that her right ear is larger than her right ear lobe, must we say that these are separate items, each of which she has pierced? By reference to the dilemma which both Pluralists and Reductive Unifiers seem to accept, why should we suppose that right lobe and right ear are distinct, in the sense that right and left ear are distinct, or else have to maintain that her right ear is identical with its lobe? Why not say her ear lobe is one constituent, among others, of her ear?

(8) THE ARGUMENT FROM SET THEORY

Pluralists and Reductive Unifiers will no doubt be unshaken. Both will probably rule that the USSR and the Socialist Republic of Great Russia are distinct, and that Jane's ear and its lobe are separate items. Hence they will say that if I attribute to each action in the BA_2-NBA_5 grouping successively more ingredient occurrences, then each must be a different performance. Actions are not sets. But we may liken deeds to collections of event-components. Then don't we have separate action-sets?

As before, I cannot envisage that BA_2 and NBA_5 are separate, in the non-trivial sense that BA_1 and BA_2 are. Furthermore, the appeal to set-theory sounds to me no more decisive than the following parallel argument:

On the track in front of railroad station R, several items of rolling stock are hitched to each other: locomotive L, coal car C, mail car M, vistadome car V and sleeping car S. A departure schedule is posted. It lists for 8 AM departure to Omaha on this track a Basic Train, composed of L and C; a Mail Train, consisting of L, C and M; a Sightseeing Special, made up of L, C, M and V; and an Overnight Express, constituted by L, C, M, V and S. No train we catalogued has exactly the same elements as any other. Accordingly, there must be

four separate trains leaving simultaneously for Omaha
on the same track of station R.

I distrust this method for increasing rail service. The
situation is not similar enough to the paradigmatic case
where you have many locomotives, each with its own cars,
lined up on the track. If Pluralists and Reductive Unifiers
were right in their application of set theory to the BA_2-
BA_5 sequence, however, it should be obvious in this
counterpart case that four separate trains are on the way
to Omaha. Since this is far from obvious, I conclude that
set theory does not resolve the issue against my view.

But is there just one train? Which one? That depends
upon your vantage point. For the engineer and his
fireman, whose reponsibilities are limited to L and C,
there is a Basic Train—with some additional cars hooked
onto it. For the postal sorter, there is a Mail Train, plus
appendages. The tired commercial traveler has a berth on
the Overnight Express. In other words, according to our
interests, we mentally divide up this collection of railroad
cars in various ways, and attach correspondingly varied
labels to it. But multiplicity of classifications does not
entail multiplicity of objects.

(9) SAME AND DIFFERENT

Opponents of my Non-Reductive Unifying position
may reformulate their grumble without set-theoretical
phraseology. Their challenge would go: Either BA_2,
NBA_2, NBA_3, NBA_4 and NBA_5 are one and the same
action, or they are different. If they are identical,
Reductive Unifiers are correct; if different, then Pluralists
win. And is there any other possibility besides one or
many, same or different? With regard to just BA_2 and

NBA_5, for example, we seem to have accepted a quartet of mutually incompatible propositions, namely:

(I)   The Prime Minister's bending his finger (BA_2) is an action he performs;

(II) His razing Dauphinia (NBA_5) is an action he performs;

(III) They are not the same action, i.e., $BA_2 \neq NBA_5$;

(IV) The Prime Minister, in carrying out BA_2 and NBA_5, does not perform different actions.

(I) and (II) are incontrovertible. (IV) seems equivalent to saying that he performed just one deed, and this raises the question: 'Which—BA_2 or NBA_5?' I want to say: Both. Yet if BA_2 and NBA_5 are not different, surely they must be identical? (see Davidson [1971], p. 20f). Not if we reconsider what (IV) means. In the context of our search for an alternative to multiplication and Reductive Unification, statement (IV) is a denial of the Pluralist's outlook. NBA_5 has components, hence spatio-temporal and other properties, not possessed by the basic action (BA_2) which is the source of NBA_5. Accordingly, NBA_5 and BA_2 are not identical. Yet I do not agree with Pluralists that these are two separate actions by the Prime Minister—in the way that BA_2 and BA_1 (his curling his lips) are two separate, numerically distinct things he does.

You may resist the idea that numerical diversity is denied in the face of compositional difference. A critic with Leibniz's Law in mind will argue that if there is a compositional difference, there must be numerical distinctness. But it is a familiar feature of physical objects which endure through time, with accretions and diminutions, that they remain the same—what?—elm tree, freight train, architectural landmark, person. I am only interested in the analogues of an object taking on broader dimensions and more parts. You can distinguish the object before and after it was augmented. But you would not automatically say, as both Reductive Unifiers and Pluralists say of basic and non-basic deed, that we have two numerically separate objects. Likewise for action. Further components are added, not to the Prime Minister's basic action of finger bending, but to the component events which have occurred already. Up until time t_3, the constituent events only amounted to the basic action of finger bending (BA_2). With E_2 at t_4, we had the non-basic performance of button-pressing (NBA_3). Five hours later, events add up to the non-basic act of destroying Dauphinia.

It is possible that I have been arguing at cross purposes about sameness and difference with Pluralists as well as Reductive Unifiers. Perhaps for both rival act-individuationists 'numerical diversity' means nothing but 'non-identity'. Both may be altogether unconcerned with the crude pre-scientific notion of numerical separability that worries me. They may disdain such unrefined questions as whether a basic action and the non-basic actions it engenders are distinct individual acts, in the sense that our Prime Minister's finger-bending is distinct from his lip-curling. Still it is a pity one finds no edification in their writings as to the difference between their lofty mathematico-set-theoretical concept of individuation, and the rustic but clear notion of numerical distinctness I have worked with. At any rate, if Pluralists or Reductive Unifiers take this 'You've misunderstood me' line, then their main debate begins to sound fairly un-momentous: Do non-basic actions have extra-bodily event components? If so, they are not identical with the basic action from which they hail; and the consequence of this will be innocuous. Non-basic actions will be distinct from their basic progenitor in the uncontroversial and unexciting sense that an ear is distinct from its lobe, the unusual sense in which four different trains are leaving simultaneously from the same track of station R for Omaha.

With regard to my crude 'separability' type of distinctness, I trust it is plain why I refuse to sunder BA_2 from NBA_5. They overlap; they share essential event components. My guiding principle is that if you set out two collection-descriptions such that some of the same elements are listed in both inventories, you have not specified two numerically distinct, separate collections. Now whatever your view of neural happenings like BP_2 and FP_2, you must allow component status to bodily motions like the bending of our protagonist's left index finger, BM_2. BM_2 seems to be on a par with the locomotive of a train. Two numerically distinct trains cannot share a single locomotive at one time; two separate actions cannot share a single bodily movement. No train without at least one locomotive; no basic or non-basic performance without some bodily goings-on, however unobtrusive.

Is there any rationale for these latter assumptions about deeds and bodily happenings? I think the no-sharing assumption is a conceptual truth, and I have already illustrated it at length. The other is necessary in respect to basic performances, but contingent for non-basic ones. Can't you imagine motorless railroad cars traveling without a locomotive to pull them? Isn't it equally conceiveable that the Prime Minister's brain processes should affect things at a distance from him, without intervening motions of his limbs? For instance, the cerebral counterpart of his desiring the red buzzer to be activated might somehow result in the buzzer's becoming compressed. But in fact bodily motions are indispensible to non-basic deeds.

(10) WHAT IS THE CAUSAL ROLE OF MENTAL ELEMENTS?

As I explained in chapters 1 through 4, my approach is compatible with dualistic and with 'identity' doctrines about the nature of beliefs, emotions and desires upon which people act. Whichever of these doctrines you espouse, you can assign a leading role to reasons for action. Either they are the same events as those neural processes which set off and regulate other bodily event components of action; or else they are non-neural but somehow causally related to those controlling brain processes.

Do our actions just happen to comprise reason components? Coordinated, goal-directed behavior seems impossible, as a matter of fact, when a person is totally unconscious or comatose. Such people just do not carry out tasks of any complexity, like robbing a bank. With rudimentary goals, perhaps it is true by definition that you must be minimally conscious when you act so as to reach or fail to reach them. I would deny that the Prime Minister pushed the red button if he lost control of his limbs during a fit of asthma. I would also deny that his fainting and collapsing unconscious upon—or near—the buzzer was touching or missing it. On the other hand, I do not require that he should be completely conscious of every detail of his bodily movements, his basic or his non-basic actions. There are always features of our current action which we ignore. When I tap my foot to some music without thinking about it, I am tapping my foot unconsciously—which is hardly to say that I am unconscious at the time! Even when I am aware of keeping time to the music, I may not realize how noisy my tapping is. So I unknowingly make a loud tapping on the floor. Similarly with reasons for action which fall on the 'volitional' side. Not wanting to, I upset the coffee pot as I reach out for it. It is just as true that I knocked it over as that I reached for it, although I only desired to do the latter. Hence we say that I overturned it—but quite unintentionally. This case also illustrates how my action may fall short of my goal. When I reached for the coffee jug, I wanted to get hold of it and pour some of its contents into my cup. Since it spilled on the table, one intention on which I acted went unfulfilled. Nevertheless that frustrated purpose was an element of my behavior.

I suppose that we consider some mental elements logically indispensable to all actions because we have established, by empirical methods, that basic and non-basic performances of any complexity go awry when appropriate states of consciousness and conation are absent. But this speculation is irrelevant to my component analysis.

One last and perhaps repetitious word about reasons. Besides being uncommitted on whether mental elements of action are identical with brain-process components, my analysis leaves you free to give any reasonable reply to the question: 'Are mental elements of action themselves things you do?' It sounds rather odd to say you engage in acts of believing, guessing, fearing, hating and lusting. Deciding is an intermediate case. But if you must talk this way, you should be on guard against infinite regresses. You should avoid implying that people have reasons for engaging in acts of believing and so on.

Since this problem is not my concern, I'll let mental activists chart ways around the regress trap. More objections to the component approach await me.

(11) WHAT QUALIFIES MENTAL AND OTHER OCCURRENCES FOR ELEMENTHOOD?

From the moment I introduced the notion of componency,

neglecting the shopworn apparatus of logically necessary and sufficient conditions, I am sure axiomatically-minded philosophers of action have wanted to put out this dialectical roadblock. Their grumble would be that I have only furnished illustrations from within and outside the sphere of human behavior. Evidently I want to contrast ingredient events with mere temporal and spatial slices or segments of a broader occurrence. Another obvious contrast would be with causes and effects of an action, which must extend beyond it in space or time. But shouldn't I also have a definition of componency, or at least criteria, to back up my examples? What if people disagree about whether a certain event is an element of some act? A short answer is that my approach will be sufficiently justified if it offers a meaningful alternative to the more implausible claims of Pluralists and Reductive Unifiers, while preserving insights of both. Until I run into serious difficulties about whether some event is or is not a constituent of a person's basic or non-basic deed, I shall avoid system-building.

We have seen that a bodily motion component, or its skeletal and muscular stand-ins, must as a matter of fact occupy a central position. Reasons belong because they enable us to specify the agent's purpose in what he did, to classify some component results as unintended, or contrary to his purpose; and because reasons help produce the bodily motion component. We noticed in Chapter 4, section (3), that reasons you have long before your body starts moving should not qualify as elements of your later deed. Although the Prime Minister's decision a week earlier may be a cause of his being resolved at t_1, and therefore a cause of his finger moving at t_2 (BM_2), I cannot give his antecedent decision component status. More generally, if I allow just any cause of the present bodily motion to be a component of what someone is doing now,

I shall find myself conceding that his action began long before he was conceived. For events which predate one's birth surely influence one's present deliberations and acts.

Along the same lines, we might wonder if we should rank just any thought, emotion or desire which coincides with bodily motion, perhaps affecting it, as a constituent of one's basic deed. What about beliefs, moods and urges which arise in us because of intervention by the proverbial mad scientist, hypnotist or witch? For example, imagine that our Prime Minister is hooked up to electrodes, laboring under a post-hypnotic suggestion or a spell. This results in an overpowering urge on his part to strike the red button; and his urge causes appropriate motion of his finger (BM_2). Did he act? In this case, I see no grounds to withhold the title of action. Unusual behavior, no doubt; and because of its origin, he should not be held legally or morally responsible. But I think it is correct to report that he performed BA_2 through NBA_5—under hypnosis or whatnot, to be sure.

Another sort of case is where the agent's desire, emotion or thought, whatever its origin, produces 'involuntary' motions like tremors, dilation of his eye pupils, perspiration, blushing or increased flow of adrenalin. Should these bodily phenomena qualify as components of his basic action? We must distinguish two situations. (i) Another bodily motion also takes place, which is agreed to be under the agent's control. I shall return to the notion of control in sections (10) and (11). For the present, I would treat a person's 'voluntary' bodily motion as defining what type of basic action he performed. In that situation, tremors would be further accidental bodily motion components of his basic action, perhaps giving it an important secondary characteristic, like the hypnotic trance in our previous case. We might say of the Prime Minister: "He shakily bent his finger". No 'manner' adverbs happen to correspond to pupil dilation and adrenalin flow. (ii) Now consider situations where no bodily motion occurs which is under the agent's control, but his desire, mood or thought produces involuntary motions (*pace* Davidson; see chapter 4, section (1)). I would deny that he has carried out a basic deed. If our Prime Minister had reached his decision, several hours before t_1, and the only observable result is his trembling, our active voice report, "He trembled", does not mark an act. This holds even if the Prime Minister welcomed his tremors, taking them as proof that he is a sensitive man. But what if, before they began, he hoped desperately for tremors, and they resulted from his longing? Then it sounds to me as if he had power over them without knowing so.

One last type of case remains. An involuntary motion takes place, or for that matter a motion which is normally under the agent's control, but he is not in a mental state which could have caused the motion. For instance, a victim of heat-stroke is comatose. He perspires and shudders. His toes wiggle and his eyelids flutter. Why do these bodily happenings not qualify as components of appropriate basic actions by the unconscious man? A high-handed 'stipulative' reply would be that I simply define all forms of action as having a mental element, hence including minimal consciousness, and require that central bodily motion components result from such happenings within the agent's mind. A more discursive answer is that such stipulations correspond to the practice of some neurophysiologists, who may differentiate voluntary from involuntary motions by reference to their diverse neural beginnings (see Vaughan [1968]). For example, certain brain events are responsible for muscle spasms, palsy and other happenings we are unable to control. Quite different processes are observed within the cortex of someone who has command over his limbs, and is successfully engaged in a course of planned activity.

Another reason why we should require that each principal bodily motion component should result from a mental element is that we can take a similar line toward another sort of challenge. I turn to it.

(12) INDIRECTLY MOVING PART OF ONE'S BODY

Although I consider it a virtue that my component approach does not extend basic actions beyond the agent's body, I do not want to rank every performance which involves *no more* than his body as a basic deed. Here is the sort of case I worry about. Suppose that our Prime Minister's left index finger is paralysed from a recent stroke. But for the same reasons I cited in the original story (RFA_2, etc.), plus the superstitious belief that using his left index finger will bring him good luck, he takes the disabled left digit between his right thumb and index, then presses it against the red buzzer. *Touching* the button with his left index (NBA_2) and the rest will quite properly remain non-basic performances. The snag for me, however, is that my approach so far would seem to require that I chalk it up as a basic deed when the Prime Minister bends his left index finger with his right hand. For doesn't the undertaking consist of a motion of his own body (BM_2), caused ultimately by his current attitudes (RFA_2 and so on)?

Intuitively speaking, the new performance does not seem basic. So my problem is to set out additional criteria which explain why it is non-basic. One method would be to lay down a distinction between principal and secondary bodily-motion components of a basic deed, and to rule that for any event to qualify as principal bodily-motion component, it may not result from another simultaneous basic action by the same agent. Since the movement of our Prime Minister's left index finger (BM_2), in the new story I imagined, does result from his basic action with his right thumb and forefinger, it (BM_2) cannot be the principal bodily-motion component of any basic action by the Prime Minister. Consequently the revised narrative does not after all record a basic action, but a non-basic one.

A complementary strategy against this trick example would be to call one last time upon our guardian neurophysiologist. Surely he can point to some observable difference between the motion of our protagonist's left index finger in the two alternative situations. Then we could say that only motions which resemble that of the original case will rank as bodily-motion components of a basic action. At the very least, our neurophysiologist can distinguish the movements of the Prime Minister's left index in the two cases by reference to their direct or indirect causal relationship to their common neural source: the cerebral process (BP_2) which sparks them in both situations.

I could also appeal to the obscure notion of an agent having control over a bodily motion. That is, I could require that whenever a basic action occurs, its bodily-motion component must be a motion of some part of the agent's body over which he is exercising control. In the trick situation I sketched, of course the Prime Minister exercises 'indirect' control over his paralysed finger. So should we rule that he must have power to move the bodily part 'directly', whenever a motion of it constitutes the bodily-motion component of a basic action? This procedure may be either unilluminating or else circular: unilluminating if we say that a man has direct control over part of his body just in case it moves the way he wants it to move whenever he pleases; and circular if we go on to define 'direct control over a part of one's anatomy' as one's power to carry out basic actions involving that part.

All these three lines of reply to the puzzle case are inconclusive. But they do reveal significant differences between what happens in the new puzzle situation and what transpires in clear examples of basic action like the finger bending in our original anecdote. Furthermore, the case of someone 'indirectly' moving a paralysed digit should provoke us to investigate what it means in action theory to speak of part of someone's body figuring in his basic performance.

(13) WHAT IS MY CRITERION FOR SAYING SOMETHING IS PART OF AN AGENT'S BODY?

In dealing with the above trick example I took it for granted that paralysed limbs belong to one's body. But another line of resistance to my component approach proves that my 'limits of the body' distinction between basic and non-basic performances must hinge upon a vague concept of corporeal boundaries. How would I classify non-organic extensions like false teeth and mechanical limbs? Will their motions qualify as bodily-movement components of basic or of non-basic activity? I suppose the same quandary would arise if these extensions were made of living material—perhaps until technologists make one's blood circulate through them. For I see no whacking difference between the way adept people manage such prosthetic devices and the way they move the limbs they are born with. But on the other side, nothing distinguishes a 'basic' seeming prosthetic device from instruments like crutches, skis and pliers, which evidently figure only in non-basic deeds. I have been informed that in earlier English law wounding someone with a prosthetic limb counted as wounding with a weapon. However, there seem to be no cases of someone with dentures biting into his victim and being accused of assault with a deadly weapon! At all events, the riddle for component theorists would be quite down to earth: Is gnashing one's false teeth a basic action? If it is, then why do we intuitively regard waving one's crutches as non-basic? False teeth and crutches are both detachable. Is it germane that dentures resemble, and fulfill the function of, bodily parts we possess from birth? Then what do we say about unorthodox-looking mechanical limbs and replacements for teeth? I have no firm answers. These obscurities merit further inquiry. But however recalcitrant they may be, I doubt that they suffice to prove I should not draw the basic/non-basic distinction at the frontiers of an agent's body—wherever one decices they belong. Like territorial waters, perhaps bodily limits are determined by flexible pragmatic considerations which other recent philosophers have investigated thoroughly, and which therefore need not detain us here.

Yet I must take time to assess another illuminating objection which might be brought against my component analysis of basic and non-basic action.

(14) CAN I ACCOUNT FOR INFERENCES FROM NON-BASIC TO BASIC ACTION SENTENCES?

This challenge goes beyond charges of incoherence, falsity or obscurity against my particular component theory. It also brings us back to the Pluralist-Reductive Unifier quarrel over individuation. Donald Davidson has formulated a general inference requirement which he thinks any analysis of action sentences ought to meet. The Pluralistic interpretation seems to fail, while Davidson's own Reductive Unifying program satisfies it. Oversimplifying, and in

my own terminology, Davidson's demand comes to this:
One's theory of how to individuate a basic action, and the
non-basic performances generated therefrom, must
explain why, for example, a relational non-basic action
sentence like 'Sebastian strolled just once through the
streets of Bologna at 2 a.m.' entails a sentence like
'Sebastian strolled.' Although it might be debatable, I
shall assume that the sentence 'Sebastian strolled' records
a basic performance. Again oversimplifying, I think
Davidson would insist that my Non-Reductive individuation theory should "mirror the patent syntactical
fact that the entailed sentence is contained in the entailing
sentence" ([1969], p. 219). I noted (sections (4) through
(9)) that, on a non-trivial interpretation, Pluralists seem to
regard these sentences as narrating quite separate
actions—for instance, because the non-basic action
sentence relates the walk to a large city (see Goldman
[1970], pp. 28–30; Thomson [1971a], p. 779; Davidson
[1969], p. 223, [1971a], p. 346). Consequently Pluralists
have to make it clear how a sentence recording one deed
can entail a sentence recording a separate deed. Pluralists
seem forced to manufacture *ad hoc* rules for each kind of
action-sentence and its entailments. Thus Goldman
declares:

> the two sentences . . . ascribe different act types to
> Sebastian. However, nobody can exemplify the first of
> these act types without examplifying the second at the
> same time ([1971], p. 770).

On Davidson's Reductive Unifying theory, Sebastian's
non-basic early morning walk through Bologna slims
down; it is numerically identical with the unique basic
action of Sebastian's which is a stroll, which takes place in
Bologna, and which occurs at 2 a.m. By Simplification,

what we might call a conjunctive non-basic action sentence here entails the basic action sentence 'Sebastian strolled.'

I cannot grumble at this feature of the Reductive Unifying analysis. But my account satisfies the inference requirement nearly as well, thus apparently doing better than a Pluralistic view. And my account will not compress relational non-basic performances, like a stroll through Bologna, or causal and conventional non-basic deeds, into the basic act from which they spring.

For the sake of completeness, I suppose I should illustrate my 'component' parsing of Davidson's two sentences. In quasi-English, I would transmute his non-basic action sentence into the following conjunction: 'A unique process occurs in Sebastian's brain (BPs); his mind is in a unique conative state (RFAs); a unique set of feed-back processes occurs in his nervous system (FPs); there are unique contractions of his muscles (MCs); a unique series of movements of his legs occurs (BMs); there is a unique traversing of the streets of Bologna (RCs); and all the foregoing events occur at 2 a.m.' My ritualistic adjective 'unique' is intended to guarantee that just one occurrence matches each conjunct of this long sentence cataloguing what happened in and around Sebastian as he ventured through Bologna at 2 a.m. With or without such litanies, it should be evident how my component reading of Davidson's non-basic action sentence allows us to infer that Sebastian strolled, *tout court*. We merely deduce the first five conjuncts of the longer sentence—which list the principal components of Sebastian's basic stroll. This procedure also permits me to agree with Reductive Unifiers that just one action has been reported. However, I need not concur that this one action must be Sebastian's basic performance of strolling *tout court*. I admit that this is one way you can report the sub-events BPs through BMs. But you can also bring in the relational sub-event

RCs and count the whole sequence as a non-basic pereg-
rination through Bologna. I have made it abundantly clear
why this flexible approach would not commit me to recog-
nizing separate, tandem basic and non-basic performances
by Sebastian.

So much for meeting Davidson's inference requirement.
This is one more benefit I can claim for a Non-Reductive
component analysis. Here is a brief résumé of those
dividends: My approach yields a straightforward account
of the relationships between basic and non-basic actions.
It enables us to avoid *prima facie* unwelcome consequences of Pluralistic as well as Reductive Unifying
theories of the basic/non-basic distinction. Yet it incorporates the Pluralist's insistence that non-basic actions go
beyond basic deeds, and also the Reductive Unifier's contentions that non-basic performances require no further
effort, and that they are not extra capers alongside one's
bodily movement. A component analysis permits us to
make distinctions of quality and spatio-temporal extent,
but without supposing that we have numerically separate
basic and non-basic actions. In addition, it provides some
enlightenment regarding the familiar but obscure notions
of doing one thing as a means of doing another, and of
causing some event to occur by performing a bodily movement. Finally, the component scheme sets aside a place of
honor for puzzling mental, neural, muscular and other
occurrences within with agent when he acts.

If we add this progress on basic and non-basic action to
whatever clarity we gained in chapters 1 through 4, then
we must conclude that the constituent analysis is a
serviceable philosophical gimmick. The ten mysterious
events we dealt with in those previous chapters are: the
brain processes which occur during sense-perception; the
alleged appearance of sense data before a percipient's

mind; the presence of objects that we see, which is supposed to cause us to see them (chapter 1); our thinking when we undergo emotions; our pleasures and other emotions which are somehow 'based' on false beliefs (chapter 2); the event of our having reasons on which we are action (chapter 3); our actions themselves and the concurrent movements of our bodies; the contractions of our muscles when we do something; and those neural goings-on which seem to determine what we do (chapter 4).

(15) EPILOGUE: DOES A COMPONENT ANALYSIS REVEAL WHAT IT IS TO ACT?

Is a component theory good for more than untangling the knots just mentioned? In calling it an "analysis" of the events we puzzled over—perception, emotion, action—do we imply that it can "lay bare the nature, or ontological status, of an act", of perceiving, of undergoing emotion? (Goldman [1971], p. 768). When I touched on similar questions before in my prefatory remarks, quoting the same words, I explained that my component theory does not disclose what it is for something to be an event. I take a broad notion of 'event' for granted, and deploy it, when I struggle to understand some puzzling occurrence, to specify what subevents make up the puzzling occurrence. But that earlier reply does not *ipso facto* prevent us from claiming that a constituent theory uncovers the essence of perception, emotion and action.

For brevity, I shall only assess the analytical hypothesis that this last chapter has displayed the essence of basic action. I think that if we claim this, a new difficulty will emerge which threatens our component analysis. It is an offshoot of the old problem about the 'soft' determinist's contention that a person acts freely, and is responsible for his deed, as well as its foreseeable consequences, whenever his own beliefs and desires cause his act. Along with many other writers on freedom, Chisholm objects:

> . . . if [his] beliefs and desires caused [a murderer] to do just what he did do, then, since *they* caused it, *he* was unable to do anything other than just what he did do. It makes no difference whether the cause of the deed was internal or external; if the cause was some state or event for which the man himself was not responsible, then he was not responsible for what we have been mistakenly calling his act ([1966], p. 13).

We already saw, in the final section of chapter 4, that from the premise that a man's brain processes caused his act or bodily movement, you cannot deduce straightaway: "*he* was unable to do anything other than just what he did do". The same holds for "beliefs and desires"—which may *be*, or include, the same persisting events or states as one's cerebral processes. So we shall not elaborate, or try to dissolve, the worries about freedom and accountability that are expressed by Chisholm and other opponents of 'soft' determinism. Instead I want to show how analogous worries may plague us if we suppose that a component theory specifies the nature of basic action.

What we have, fundamentally, is a deterministic tableau. Never mind whether 'soft' or 'hard' conclusions on freedom and responsibility may be extracted from it. Suppose basic action is a sequence of events, beginning with either neural or motivational episodes, and terminating in agitation or stillness of the agent's limbs—with muscle contractions and feedback processes sandwiched in between. Where does that leave the agent? He seems to have no role. He is like an arena where 'his' calculations, his perceptual judgments, his noble and base inclinations, perhaps his repressed fantasies, his conscious terrors, rages, lusts and devotions, do all the work. They combine or clash with each other, and bring about movement of his limbs. Perhaps we are mistaken, as Chisholm insinuates, to call this sequence the agent's "act". Since everything that followed his "beliefs and desires" was merely their effect, should we not echo Chisholm's phrase: "*they caused it*"? The agent himself seems to be left out, having little to do with these events.

Some determinists—probably 'soft' ones—will remind us that, after all, it is the agent who calculates, hankers, and so on; thus we do not merely have cause-effect sequences, triggered by his "beliefs and desires", operating within the confines of his body. But this reminds me of Prichard's curious doctrine that action consists exclusively in willing. Prichard wrote:

> . . . there seems to be no resisting the conclusion that where we think of ourselves or of another as having done a certain action, the kind of activity of which we are thinking is that of willing . . . and that when we refer to some instance of this activity . . . as our having moved our finger . . . , we refer to it thus not because we think it was, or consisted in, the causing our finger to move . . . , but because we think it has a certain change of state as an effect.
> . . . When I move my hand, the movement of my hand, though an effect of my action [of willing], is not itself an action, and no one who considered the matter would say it was . . . an action or even part of an action ([1949], pp. 190f).

This doctrine puts the agent back into our deterministic scheme as a full-fledged participant. But our remodeling costs are exhorbitant; for now we can only say that an agent performs volitional stunts—or, to broaden Prichard's view, that an agent does nothing more than inaugurate his cognitive, conative and affective attitudes. In my jargon, we lose neural, muscular and large-scale bodily components of action, which will only consist of mental elements.

We can escape this 'No agency or Prichardian willing' dilemma. We simply disavow any claim to have analysed basic action—or any other kind of action—in a way that yields the 'essence' of agency. We modestly explain that, although our component story does not disclose what it is to be an agent, we have nevertheless recorded vital sub-occurrences that characterize action. In a sense, the agent himself does not figure in our narrative of what goes on when he acts. So he is neither active nor passive in the proceedings.

This latest riddle, which concerns our own theory of the elements of action, may be bogus. As I warned in the Preface, it is not my aim to prove that any of the dozen controversies I treat are genuine. Consequently I do not oppose metaphysicians who manage to head off the befuddling disputes I consider, by simply depicting basic and non-basic action, and the other eleven phenomena we have worried about, in terms that generate no puzzlement. Similarly, I have no quarrel with practitioners of alternative therapies for relieving our conceptual cramps. I have no idea whether my subdividing approach is the neatest or most satisfactory; but I am sure that it is not the only method of dealing with our riddles.

I have a hunch that there are further applications for my component analysis. Notably, it could be expanded into a general, predominantly materialistic theory of mental events. What I have said about perceiving, having sense data, thinking, undergoing emotion, and being motivated to act by a desire, decision or other conative attitude, might be the nucleus of such a global account. If Cartesians insist that I have omitted our conscious 'feelings' of rage, remorse and delight from my story of these emotions, I can add these apparently immaterial items as event-elements—as I added sense data to perceiving. The same with putative 'feelings' of lust, agressiveness, resolution and hesitancy on the conative side—and conviction or uncertainty on the cognitive. Moving on to that philosophical favourite, being in pain, I would obviously include brain-processes as an ingredient, along with cognitive elements (thinking that one's body is damaged), more encompassing emotional elements like fear, and aversive dispositions as well as overt thrashing and groaning. To satisfy Cartesians, again, I could add the 'raw feel', the supposed pain sensation of which the sufferer alone is so uncomfortably aware. But notice that we would never assimilate the overall emotion, conative attitude, thinking or pain to the allegedly characteristic 'feeling' alone. The latter would only be part of the mental event. The same holds for equating pain or any other mental occurrence with its neural event-component. Thus a component approach might reconcile various seemingly incompatible analyses of the relationship between mental and physical occurrences.

This is an inviting prospect for further detailed work. But I reiterate that it is unwise to expect the notion of event-componency, or any metaphysical concept or principle, to be a skeleton key to the whole baffling cosmos. With such reservations, I think it has proven its utility.

Bibliography

Abbreviations for Journals:

A	*Analysis*
APQ	*American Philosophical Quarterly*
IN	*Inquiry*
JP	*Journal of Philosophy*
M	*Mind*
PAS/SV	*Proceedings of the Aristotelian Society/ Supplementary Volume*
PQ	*Philosophical Quarterly*
PR	*Philosophical Review*

ANSCOMBE, G. E. M. [1957] *Intention*. Oxford: Blackwell's.

ARMSTRONG, D. M. [1968] *A Materialist Theory of Mind*. London: Routledge.

ATWELL, J. E. [1969] "The Accordion-Effect Thesis", *PQ*, XIX, pp. 337-42.

AYERS, M. R. [1970] "Perception and Action", in *Royal Institute of Philosophy Lectures*, Vol. III: 1968-9. London: Macmillan.

BAIER, Annette [1971] "The Search for Basic Actions", *APQ*, VIII, pp. 161-70.

BEDFORD, E. [1957] "Emotions", reprinted in Gustafson [1964], pp. 77-98.

BENNETT, J. [1973] "Shooting, Killing and Dying", *Canadian Journal of Philosophy*, II, pp. 315-324.

BINKLEY, R. *et al* (eds.) [1971] *Agent, Reason and Action*. Toronto: U. of Toronto Press.

BRAND, M. [1968] "Danto on Basic Actions", *Nous*, II, pp. 187–190.

—— (ed.) [1970] *The Nature of Human Action*. Glenview, III: Scott-Foresman.

BRANDT, R., and KIM, J. [1967] "The Logic of the Identity Theory", *JP*, LXIV, pp. 515–37.

BRODBECK, M. (ed.) [1968] *Readings in the Philosophy of the Social Sciences*. New York: Macmillan.

BROWN, D. G. [1968] *Action*. London: Allen and Unwin. See esp. pp. 137–9.

CHISHOLM, R. M. [1964] "The Descriptive Element in the Concept of Action", *JP*, LXI, pp. 613–625.

—— [1966] "Freedom and Action", in Lehrer (ed.), pp. 11–44.

—— [1969] "Some Puzzles About Agency", in K. Lambert (ed.), *The Logical Way of Doing Things*. New Haven: Yale U. Press, pp. 199–217.

—— [1970] "Events and Propositions", *Nous*, IV, pp. 15–24.

—— [1971] "Reflections on Human Agency", *Idealistic Studies*, I, pp. 33–45.

DANTO, A. [1963] "What We Can Do", *JP*, LX, pp. 434–45.

—— [1965] "Basic Actions", *APQ*, II, pp. 141–8.

—— [1970] "Causation and Basic Actions", *IN*, XIII, pp. 108–25.

—— [1973] *Analytical Philosophy of Action*. Cambridge: University Press.

DAVENAY, T. F. [1961] "Wanting", *PQ*, XI, pp. 135–44.

—— [1964] "Choosing", *M*, LXXIII, pp. 515–26.

—— [1966] "Intentions and Causes", *A*, XXVII, pp. 23–8.

DAVIDSON, D. [1963] "Actions, Reasons and Causes", *JP*, LX, pp. 685–700.

——[1967] "The Logical Form of Action Sentences", in Rescher [1967], pp. 81-95.

——[1969] "The Individuation of Events", in Rescher [1969], pp. 216-34.

——[1969a] "On Events and Event Descriptions", in J. Margolis, ed., *Fact and Existence*. Oxford: Blackwells, pp. 74-84.

——[1970] "Action and Reaction", *IN*, XIII, pp. 140-8.

——[1970a] "Mental Events", in Foster and Swain (eds.), *Experience and Theory*. Amherst: U. of Mass Press, pp. 79-101.

——[1970b] "Events as Particulars", *Nous*, IV, pp. 25-32.

——[1971] "Agency", in Binkley *et al* [1971], pp. 3-25.

——[1971a] "Eternal vs. Ephemeral Events", *Nous*, V, pp. 335-49.

——[1972] "Freedom to Act", in Honderich [1972], pp. 139-56.

DAVIS, L. [1970] "Individuation of Actions", *JP*, LXVII, pp. 520-32.

DENNETT, D. [1972] "Mechanism and Responsibility", in Honderich [1972], pp. 159-84.

FEINBERG, J. [1965] "Action and Responsibility", in M. Black (ed.) *Philosophy in America*. Ithaca, N.Y.: Cornell U. Press, pp. 134-60.

——[1972] *Doing and Deserving*. Princeton: University Press.

FOOT, P. [1957] "Free Will as Involving Determinism", reprinted in Morgenbesser and Walsh [1962], pp. 71-80.

GOLDMAN, A. [1970] *A Theory of Human Action*. Englewood Cliffs, N.J.: Prentice Hall.

——[1971] "The Individuation of Action", *JP*, LXVIII, pp. 761-74.

GRICE, H. P. [1961] "The Causal Theory of Perception", reprinted in Warnock [1967], pp. 85-112.

GUSTAFSON, D. (ed.) [1964] *Essays in Philosophical Phychology*. Garden City, N.Y.: Doubleday.

HAMLYN, D. W. [1953] "Behavior", *Philosophy*, XXVIII, pp. 132-45.

——[1964] "Causality and Human Behavior", *PAS/SV*, XXXVIII, pp. 125-42.

HAMPSHIRE, S. (ed.) [1966] *Philosophy of Mind*. New York: Harper and Row.

HONDERICH, T. (ed.) [1972] *Essays on Freedom of Action*. London: Routledge. Includes essay, "One Determinism", by Honderich.

KENNY, A. [1963] *Action, Emotion and Will*. London: Routledge-Kegan Paul.

KIM, J. [1966] "On the Psycho-Physical Identity Theory", *APQ*, III, pp. 227-35.

——[1973] "Causation, Nomic Subsumption, and the Concept of Event", *JP*, LXX, pp. 217-36.

——[1974]. "Noncausal Connections", *Nous*, VIII, pp. 41-52.

LEHRER, K. (ed.) [1966] *Freedom and Determinism*. N.Y.: Random House.

MACINTYRE, A. [1964] "A Mistake About Causality in Social Science", in Laslett and Runciman (eds.) *Philosophy, Politics and Society*. Oxford: Blackwell's.

MALCOLM, N. [1967] "Explaining Behavior", *PR*, LXXVI, pp. 97-104.

——[1968] "The Conceivability of Mechanism", *PR*, LXXVII, pp. 45-72.

MARGOLIS, J. [1970] "Danto on Basic Actions", *IN*, XIII, pp. 104-8.

MARTIN, R. M. [1969] "On Events and Event-Descriptions", in J. Margolis (ed.), *Fact and Existence*. Oxford: Blackwell's, pp. 63-74.

McCANN, H. [1972] "Is Raising One's Arm a Basic Action?", *JP*, LXIX, pp. 235-49.

——[1974] "Volition and Basic Action", *PR*, LXXXIII pp. 451-73.

MELDEN, A. I. [1956] "Action", reprinted in Gustafson [1964], pp. 58-73.

——[1961] *Free Action*. London: Routledge.

MORGENBESSER, S., and WALSH, J. J. (eds.) [1962] *Free Will*. Englewood Cliffs, N.J.: Prentice Hall.

OFSTAD, H. [1967] "Recent Work on the Freewill Problem", *APQ*, IV, pp. 179-207.

PEARS, D. F. [1963] Editor and contributor, *Freedom and the Will*. N.Y.: Macmillan.

——[1967] "Are Reasons for Actions Causes?" in A. Stroll (ed.) *Epistemology*. N.Y.: Harper and Row, pp. 204-28.

——[1968] "Desires as Causes of Actions", in *Royal Institute of Philosophy Lectures*, Vol. I: 1966-7. London: Macmillan.

——[1971] "Two problems about Reasons for Action", in Binkley *et al* [1971], pp. 128-53.

PENELHUM, T. [1964] "Pleasure and Falsity", reprinted in Hampshire [1966], pp. 242-65.

PETERS, R. S. [1952] "Motives and Causes", *PAS/SV*, XXVI, pp. 139-62.

——[1958] *The Concept of Motivation*. London: Routledge.

PLATO. *Philebus*. Translated by R. Hackforth. N.Y.: Liberal Arts Press, 1945.

——. *Republic*. Translated by F. M. Cornford. Oxford: University Press. See Stephanus number 587 for discussion of 'false pleasures'.

PRICHARD, H. A. [1949] *Moral Obligation*. Oxford: Clarendon Press.

RESCHER, N. (ed.) [1967] *The Logic of Decision and Action*. Pittsburgh: U. of Pittsburgh Press.

——(ed.) [1969] *Essays in Honor of Carl G. Hempel*.

Dordrecht: D. Reidel.

——[1970] "On the Characterization of Actions", in Brand [1970], pp. 247-54.

RUSSELL, B. [1927] *Outline of Philosophy*. London: Allen and Unwin.

RYLE, G. [1954] "Pleasure", reprinted in Gustafson [1964], pp. 195-205.

SHER, G. [1973] "Causal Explanation and the Vocabulary of Action", *M*, LXXXII, pp. 22-30.

SMART, J. J. C. [1959] "Sensations and Brain Processes", reprinted in C. B. Borst (ed.), *The Mind-Body Identity Theory*. N.Y.: St. Martin's, 1970, pp. 141-56.

——[1972] "Further Thoughts on the Identity Theory", *The Monist*, LVI, pp. 149-62.

STOUTLAND, F. [1970] "The Logical Connection Thesis", *APQ* Monograph 4, pp. 117-29.

STRAUDE, M. [1974] "Irving Thalberg's Component Analysis of Emotion and Action", *PQ*, XXIV, pp. 150-55.

STRAWSON, P. F. [1963] Participating in BBC discussion edited by Pears [1963].

TAYLOR, C. [1964] *The Explanation of Behavior*. London: Routledge.

TAYLOR, R. [1966] *Action and Purpose*. Englewood Cliffs: Prentice Hall.

THALBERG, I. [1962] "False Pleasures", *JP*, LIX, pp. 65-74.

——[1964] "Emotions and Thought", reprinted in Hampshire [1966], pp. 201-24.

——[1972] *Enigmas of Agency*. London: Allen and Unwin.

——[1974] Review of Wilson [1972], *PR*, LXXXIII, pp. 278-80.

THOMSON, J. J. [1971] "The Time of a Killing", *JP*, LXVIII, pp. 115-32.

——[1971a] "Individuating Actions", *JP*, LXVIII, pp. 774-81.

URMSON, J. O. [1952] "Motives and Causes", *PAS/SV*, XXVI, pp. 179-94.

VAUGHAN, H. G., Jr. [1968] "Topography of the Human Motor Potential", *EEG and Clinical Neurophysiology Journal,* XXV, pp. 1-10.

WARE, R. X. [1973] "Acts and Action", *JP*, LXX, pp. 403-18.

WARNOCK, G. J. (ed.) [1967] *The Philosophy of Perception*. Oxford: O.U.P.

WEIL, Vivian [1972] *Basic Action: A Component Analysis*. Unpublished doctoral thesis, University of Illinois at Chicago Circle.

WHITE, A. R. [1961] "The Causal Theory of Perception", reprinted in Warnock [1967], pp. 113-49.

WIGGINS, D. [1971] *Identity and Spatio-Temporal Continuity*. Oxford: Blackwell's.

WILLIAMS, B. A. O. [1959] "Pleasure and Belief", reprinted in Hampshire [1966], pp. 225-41.

WILSON, J. R. S. [1972] *Emotion-and Object*. Cambridge: University Press.

Index

Action
  Identifiable with bodily movement?, 3, 53–83
  "Ontological nature", or essence of?, 6ff., 125–128
  Principal bodily-motion component of, 66–71, 118f.
  Reasons for; how 'based' on, 2, 6, 82f., 88f., 113–18
Agency—more to it than component occurrences listed here?, 5
Anscombe, G. E. M., 131
Argument from Alternative Realizations (to prove actions "indistinguishable from bodily movements"), 62–6, 86
Argument from Set Theory (against a component analysis of basic and 'resulting' non-basic actions), 108f.
Armstrong, D. M., 32, 131
Aristotle, theory mentioned by J. J. C. Smart, 13
Atwell, J. E., 131
Ayers, M. R., 131

Baier, A., 62f., 131
Basic and non-basic action—
  Individuation problem, 4, 6, 33, 85–125
  Numerical distinctness of, 87, 99ff., 107f., 111f., 117, 123f.

Temporal dimensions of, 98–101
Bedford, E., 32, 131
Belief—
  As ingredient of perceiving, 19, 28; of action, 46; of emotion, 31
Bennett, J., 131
Binkley, R., 132
'Bodily Motion' Argument of entailment theorists, 45ff., 48
"Bodily movement": ambiguity of notion; active or transitive, and non-committal senses of, 58, 60
Body, limits of, 86, 92, 98, 120f.
Brain processes, 1, 3, 4, 12–20, 34, 39f., 64, 71–83, 88f., 94, 119, 126
  Not all there is to mental events, 128f.
Brand, M., 132
Brandt, R., and J. Kim, 7, 132
Brodbeck, M., 132
Brown, D. G., 132

Causation—
  Backwards?, 3, 67, 69
  Temporal aspects of, 101–105
Chisholm, R. M., vi, 56, 67, 126f., 132
Components—
  Causal, 16ff., (versus causes of the occurrence, 17, 30, 66)